Dr. C. White-Elliott

CLF Publishing, LLC.
9161 Sierra Ave, Ste. 203C
Fontana, CA 92335
www.clfpublishing.org

Copyright © 2017 by Cassundra White-Elliott. All rights reserved. No portion of this book may be reproduced, stored in a retrieval system, or transmitted by any form or any means electronically, photocopied, recorded, or any other except for brief quotations in printed reviews, without the prior permission of the publisher.

Cover design by *Senir Design*. Contact information- info@senirdesign.com.

ISBN # 978-1-9451022-2-6

Printed in the United States of America.

Table of Contents

Grammar Workbook 5

Comprehensive Test 7

Commonly Confused Words 11

Understanding Punctuation 15

    Apostrophe 17

    Quotation Marks 21

    Hyphen 23

Pronoun Agreement 27

Dangling & Misplaced Modifiers 37

Active vs Passive Voice 41

Parts of Speech Guidelines 45

101+ Power Verbs 51

Twelve Common Writing Errors 59

Essentials of Business Writing Workbook 63

Fundamentals of Business Writing 65

Oral vs Written Communication 69

Misplaced & Dangling Modifiers 73

Business Letter 77

Business Memos 83

Professional Emails 89

Proofreading 97

Grammar Workbook

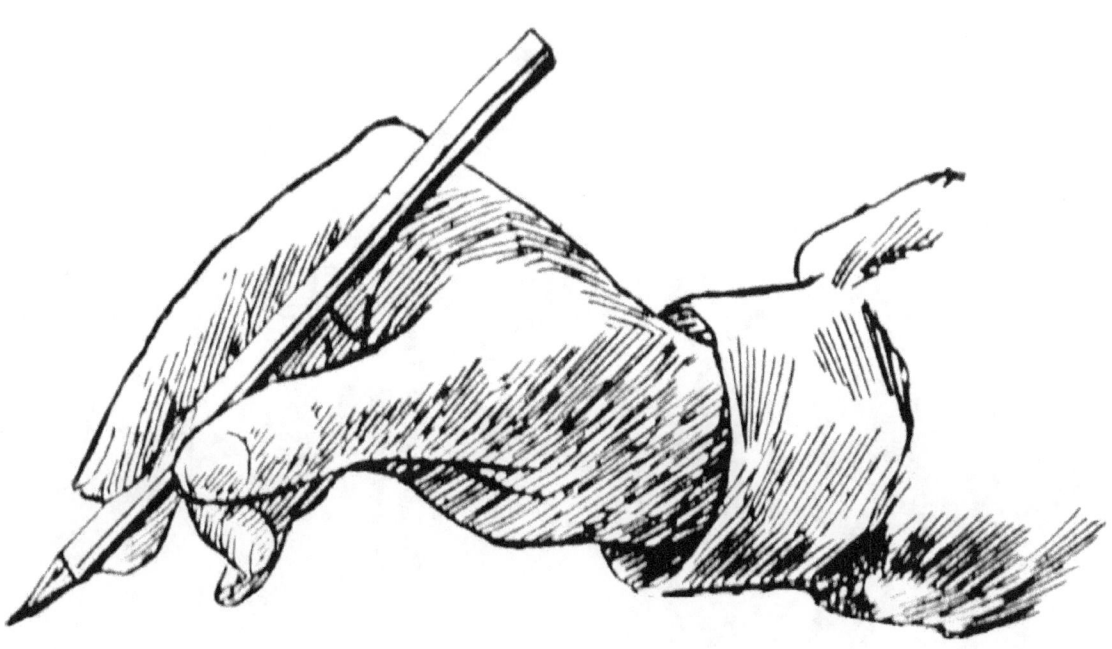

COMPREHENSIVE TEST

(Grammar, Spelling, & Punctuation)

Comprehensive Grammar, Spelling, and Punctuation Test

Try your hand at the following comprehensive grammar, spelling, and punctuation test.

Part A: Revision

Rewrite the sentences below by fixing the errors, which may be in spelling, grammar, punctuation, or any combination of the three. Every sentence has at least one error, though most sentences have several errors.

1. The short story Where Are You Going, Where Have You Been is a brilliant masterful work that examines the life of the Modern American Teenager.

2. William Faulkners' style is often compared to Ernest Hemingways'; because both writers employ the modern, technique stream of consciousness

3. The beautiful interesting novel had a brilliance about it I had never experienced, it truly touched me.

4. When I was in Europe I learned that other cultures view Americans and our ideas as hedonistic yet they also see Americans as hip modern and idealistic.

5. Neil Postman writes about this problem, in his seminal, book "Amusing Ourselves to Death": Everything in our background has prepared us to know and resist a prison when the gates begin to close around us.. But who is prepared to take arms against a sea of amusements? To whom do we complain….when serious discourse dissolves into giggles?'.

6. My Philosophy Professor announced, "Today we will address Thoreau's statement, "the price of anything is the amount of life you exchange for it.

7. The best teacher, we ever had, Mrs. Meyer told us never give up on your dream.

8. Thomas could be a brilliant writer, he just does not know it because he spends too much time, watching Television.

9. Smith's report defines "sustainable development" as "development that meets the needs of the present without compromising the ability of future generations to meet their own needs. Smith's definition is important to consider because it illustrates that that we do not have to destroy the natural environment, to have economic progress.

10. We had a pretty impressive guest list for the party, we invited Tom Stoppard, Playwright, J.K. Rowling, Author, and Ron Howard, Director.

11. David, my friend from work told me you are never going to get anywhere unless you believe in yourself.'

12. A government, ruled solely or mostly by a single individual, is a dictatorship.

13. There are three basic, economic systems present within modern nations; capitalism socialism and communism.

14. The bureaucracy of Higher Education can be overwhelming, just remember to remain calm be polite and ask questions about anything you do not understand.

15. Be careful what you Post about your Classes on facebook or twitter. It is not wise to tweet rude; judgmental thoughts about your class the material or the Professor online where anyone can read it. Remember; professors are active on Social Networks; too.

16. Mrs. Hall, my school librarian always told us, 'Be careful what you think about yourself; for you will become what you think'.

17. Staring in is Spring Semester my Cousin and I will be taking Philosophy Biology and English.

18. One of the most beautiful cities in the world is San Francisco California, it is widely known for its majestic; views and rolling, hills.

19. Most readers usually miss the full significance of Shakespeares' play "Hamlet"; because they often believe its simply a play about revenge.

Part B: Spelling and Usage
Circle the correct usage of the underlined words in the sentences below.

20. We had fewer/less items than the allowed limit, so we were able to use the express line where there are fewer/less people waiting.

21. I thought about stealing the money, but I knew my conscious/conscience would bother me if I did; even if I was never caught, I would always be conscious/conscience of my theft.

22. There/they're/their were so many things I wanted to say to him, but since his friends were there/ they're/their, I said nothing and just waited for there/they're/their departure.

23. Its/It's true that some readers have scene/seen the poem as pedantic, but I thought the work and its/it's message were important and interesting.

24. The very site/cite/sight of the book is enough to bring tears to my eyes; its/it's cover and language are so beautiful that in every paper I write, I feel compelled to cite/sight/site an excerpt from it.

25. Whomever/whoever wins the lottery will be a multimillionaire; I hope he or she will remember all those who/whom have been good to them.

26. My older sister is taller than I/me. Please RSVP to the party by sending an e-mail to Silas or I/me.

27. I finally gained access/excess/assess/except to the website with my log-in information, but once I logged in, I could not access/excess/assess/except how well I was doing with the assigned work.

28. How much farther/further will we have to drive in this car? I could not read his hand-drawn map, so I asked him to explain it to me farther/further.

29. I feel good/well today; I think I did very good/well on my test.

COMMONLY CONFUSED WORDS

Words Commonly Confused Worksheet

Part 1: For each of the following sentences, circle the word or words that best complete the sentence correctly.

1. I couldn't decide (which / witch) color shoes I wanted.

2. If a cat falls (of / off) the counter, it will land on its feet.

3. Make sure you do (your / you're) homework right after school.

4. I talked (to / too / two) my brother yesterday.

5. (Are / Our) you going to be on (are / our) baseball team?

6. He bought (to / too / two) speakers (to / too / two) complete his stereo system.

7. I saw (their / there / they're) mom sitting (their / there / they're).

8. I think (their / there / they're) in trouble!

9. New surgeries for blind people can restore (their / there / they're) sight.

10. The dog chewed on (its / it's) squeaky toy.

11. My neighbor dressed as a (which / witch) for Halloween.

12. She couldn't remember (were / where) she had put her purse.

13. I would rather be poor and happy (than / then) rich and sad.

14. Do you think (its / it's) going to rain?

15. (Know No), you may not go to that concert unless (your / you're) 18.

16. After practice, I walked (strait / straight) to my bed, (to / too) tired to eat.

17. (Were / Where) you scared during the movie at all?

18. Clean your room, and (than / then) you may watch TV.

19. The site of the new shopping mall will be over (their / there / they're).

20. (Which / Witch) (of / off) them do you want?

21. I (hear / here) that you've won a trip to Europe.

22. I do not (no / know) the answer to this problem.

23. I'm not sure (weather / whether) it will rain this weekend or not.

24. My friends have seen me (threw / through) some difficult times.

25. She was (quiet / quite) surprised by her birthday present.

26. If the (weather / whether) is bad, we will have to cancel our camping trip.

27. In study hall, all students must be (quiet / quite).

28. He (threw / through) the ball right (hear / here) and broke a car window.

Part 2: Circle the misused words in the paragraph below. Above the error, write the correct word choice.

In Cambodia, around 55 miles north of Phnom Phen, tarantula spiders our commonly eaten by the locals, but travelers who pass threw often try them, to. (Would you take a bite of one? I don't no weather I would or not. I'd have too be starving! Maybe their better then worms, though.) The practice began in the days of the Khmer Rouge when food was to scarce and the people where hungry. But apparently the locals developed a taste for the furry eight-legged arachnids, and now their a major part of the town's dietary intake. According too the people who eat spiders, there quiet good! Hundreds of spiders are hunted, cooked, and sold every day in what must be one of the more unusual 'fast food' arrangements in the world.

Part 3: On the bottom of this page, write one sentence for each set of words, underlining each commonly confused word. (You may write more than one sentence per set if needed.)

Example: I'm quite excited that the students are quiet today so we can all write!

1. (were, where, we're)

2. (its, it's)

3. (your, you're)

4. (there, their, they're)

5. (to, too, two)

6. (then, than)

UNDERSTANDING PUNCTUATION

Quick Guide to Commas

1. Use commas to separate independent clauses when they are joined by any of these seven coordinating conjunctions: *and, but, for, or, nor, so, yet.*

2. Use commas after introductory a) clauses, b) phrases, or c) words that come before the main clause.

3. Use a pair of commas in the middle of a sentence to set off clauses, phrases, and words that are not essential to the meaning of the sentence. Use one comma before to indicate the beginning of the pause and one at the end to indicate the end of the pause.

4. Do not use commas to set off essential elements of the sentence, such as clauses beginning with *that* (relative clauses). *That* clauses after nouns are always essential. *That* clauses following a verb expressing mental action are always essential.

5. Use commas to separate three or more words, phrases, or clauses written in a series.

6. Use commas to separate two or more coordinate adjectives that describe the same noun. Be sure never to add an extra comma between the final adjective and the noun itself or to use commas with non-coordinate adjectives.

7. Use a comma near the end of a sentence to separate contrasted coordinate elements or to indicate a distinct pause or shift.

8. Use commas to set off phrases at the end of the sentence that refer back to the beginning or middle of the sentence. Such phrases are free modifiers that can be placed anywhere in the sentence without causing confusion.

9. Use commas to set off all geographical names, items in dates (except the month and day), addresses (except the street number and name), and titles in names.

10. Use a comma to shift between the main discourse and a quotation.

The Apostrophe

The apostrophe has three uses:

1. To form possessives of nouns

2. To show the omission of letters

3. To indicate certain plurals of lowercase letters

Forming Possessives of Nouns

To see if you need to make a possessive, turn the phrase around and make it an "of the..." phrase.

For example:

    the boy's hat = the hat of the boy

    three days' journey = journey of three days

If the noun after "of" is a building, an object, or a piece of furniture, then **no** apostrophe is needed!

room of the hotel = hotel room

door of the car = car door

leg of the table = table leg

Once you've determined whether you need to make a possessive, follow these rules to create one.

- **add 's to the singular form of the word (even if it ends in -s):**

the owner's car

James's hat (James' hat is also acceptable. For plural, proper nouns that are possessive, use an apostrophe after the 's': "The Eggleses' presentation was good." The Eggleses are a husband and wife consultant team.)

- **add 's to the plural forms that do not end in -s:**

the children's game

the geese's honking

- add ' to the end of plural nouns that end in -s:

two cats' toys

three friends' letters

the countries' laws

- add 's to the end of compound words:

my brother-in-law's money

- add 's to the last noun to show joint possession of an object:

Todd and Anne's apartment

Showing omission of letters

Apostrophes are used in contractions. A contraction is a word (or set of numbers) in which one or more letters (or numbers) have been omitted. The apostrophe shows this omission.

Contractions are common in speaking and in informal writing. To use an apostrophe to create a contraction, place an apostrophe where the omitted letter(s) would go. Here are some examples:

don't = do not

I'm = I am

he'll = he will

who's = who is

shouldn't = should not

didn't = did not

could've = could have (NOT "could of"!)

'60 = 1960

Forming plurals of lowercase letters

Apostrophes are used to form plurals of letters that appear in lowercase; here the rule appears to be more typographical than grammatical, e.g. "three ps" versus "three p's." To form the plural of a lowercase letter, place **'s** after the letter. There is no need for apostrophes indicating a plural on capitalized letters, numbers, and symbols (though keep in mind that some editors, teachers, and professors still prefer them). Here are some examples:

p's and q's = minding your p's and q's is a phrase believed to be taken from the early days of the printing press when letters were set in presses backwards so they would appear on the printed page correctly. Although the origins of this phrase are disputed, the expression was used commonly to mean, "Be careful, don't make a mistake." Today, the term also indicates maintaining politeness, possibly from "mind your pleases and thank-yous."

Nita's mother constantly stressed minding one's p's and q's.

three Macintosh G4s = three of the Macintosh model G4

There are three G4s currently used in the writing classroom.

many &s = many ampersands

That printed page has too many &s on it.

the 1960s = the years in decade from 1960 to 1969

The 1960s were a time of great social unrest.

The '60s were a time of great social unrest.

Don't use apostrophes for personal pronouns, the relative pronoun *who*, or for noun plurals.

Apostrophes should not be used with possessive pronouns because possessive pronouns already show possession—they don't need an apostrophe. His, her, its, my, yours, ours are all possessive pronouns. However, indefinite pronouns, such as one, anyone, other, no one, and anybody, can be made possessive. Here are some examples:

INCORRECT: **his'** book

CORRECT: **his** book

CORRECT: **one's** book

CORRECT: **anybody's** book

INCORRECT: **Who's** dog is this?

CORRECT: **Whose** dog is this?

INCORRECT: The group made **it's** decision.

CORRECT: The group made **its** decision.

(Note: *Its* and *it's* are not the same thing. *It's* is a contraction for "it is" and *its* is a possessive pronoun meaning "belonging to it." It's raining out = it is raining out. A simple way to remember this rule is the fact that you don't use an apostrophe for the possessive his or hers, so don't do it with its!)

INCORRECT: a friend of **yours'**

CORRECT: a friend of **yours**

Using Quotation Marks

The primary function of quotation marks is to set off and represent exact language (either spoken or written) that has come from somebody else. The quotation mark is also used to designate speech acts in fiction and sometimes poetry. Since you will most often use them when working with outside sources, successful use of quotation marks is a practical defense against accidental plagiarism and an excellent practice in academic honesty. The following rules of quotation mark use are the standard in the United States, although it may be of interest that usage rules for this punctuation do vary in other countries.

The following covers the basic use of quotation marks. For details and exceptions consult the separate sections of this guide.

Direct Quotations

Direct quotations involve incorporating another person's exact words into your own writing.

1. Quotation marks always come in pairs. Do not open a quotation and fail to close it at the end of the quoted material.

2. Capitalize the first letter of a direct quote when the quoted material is a complete sentence.

Mr. Johnson, who was working in his field that morning, said, "The alien spaceship appeared right before my own two eyes."

3. Do not use a capital letter when the quoted material is a fragment or only a piece of the original material's complete sentence.

Although Mr. Johnson has seen odd happenings on the farm, he stated that the spaceship "certainly takes the cake" when it comes to unexplainable activity.

4. If a direct quotation is interrupted mid-sentence, do not capitalize the second part of the quotation.

"I didn't see an actual alien being," Mr. Johnson said, "but I sure wish I had."

5. In all the examples above, note how the period or comma punctuation always comes before the final quotation mark. It is important to realize also that when you are using MLA or some other form of documentation, this punctuation rule may change.

When quoting text with a spelling or grammar error, you should transcribe the error exactly in your own text. However, also insert the term sic in italics directly after the mistake, and enclose it in brackets. Sic is from the Latin, and translates to "thus," "so," or "just as that." The word tells the reader that your quote is an exact reproduction of what you found, and the error is not your own.

Mr. Johnson says of the experience, "It's made me reconsider the existence of extraterestials [*sic*]."

6. Quotations are most effective if you use them sparingly and keep them relatively short. Too many quotations in a research paper will get you accused of not producing original thought or material (they may also bore a reader who wants to know primarily what YOU have to say on the subject).

Indirect Quotations

Indirect quotations are not exact wordings but rather rephrasings or summaries of another person's words. In this case, it is not necessary to use quotation marks. However, indirect quotations still require proper citations, and you will be commiting plagiarism if you fail to do so.

Mr. Johnson, a local farmer, reported last night that he saw an alien spaceship on his own property.

Many writers struggle with when to use direct quotations versus indirect quotations. Use the following tips to guide you in your choice.

Use direct quotations when the source material uses language that is particularly striking or notable. Do not rob such language of its power by altering it.

Martin Luther King Jr. believed that the end of slavery was important and of great hope to millions of slaves done horribly wrong.

The above should never stand in for:

Martin Luther King Jr. said of the Emancipation Proclamation, "This momentous decree came as a great beacon light of hope to millions of Negro slaves who had been seared in the flames of withering injustice."

Use an indirect quotation (or paraphrase) when you merely need to summarize key incidents or details of the text.

Use direct quotations when the author you are quoting has coined a term unique to her or his research and relevant within your own paper.

Hyphen Use

Two words brought together as a compound may be written separately, written as one word, or connected by hyphens. For example, three modern dictionaries all have the same listings for the following compounds:

hair stylist

hairsplitter

hair-raiser

Another modern dictionary, however, lists hairstylist, not hair stylist. Compounding is obviously in a state of flux, and authorities do not always agree in all cases, but the uses of the hyphen offered here are generally agreed upon.

    1. Use a hyphen to join two or more words serving as a single adjective before a noun:

a one-way street

chocolate-covered peanuts

well-known author

However, when compound modifiers come after a noun, they are not hyphenated:

The peanuts were chocolate covered.

The author was well known.

    2. Use a hyphen with compound numbers:

forty-six

sixty-three

Our much-loved teacher was sixty-three years old.

    3. Use a hyphen to avoid confusion or an awkward combination of letters:

re-sign a petition (vs. resign from a job)

semi-independent (but semiconscious)

shell-like (but childlike)

    4. Use a hyphen with the prefixes ex- (meaning former), self-, all-; with the suffix -elect; between a prefix and a capitalized word; and with figures or letters:

ex-husband

self-assured

mid-September

all-inclusive

mayor-elect

anti-American

T-shirt

pre-Civil War

mid-1980s

5. Use a hyphen to divide words at the end of a line if necessary, and make the break only between syllables:

pref-er-ence

sell-ing

in-di-vid-u-al-ist

6. For line breaks, divide already-hyphenated words only at the hyphen:

mass-

produced

self-

conscious

7. For line breaks in words ending in -ing, if a single final consonant in the root word is doubled before the suffix, hyphenate between the consonants; otherwise, hyphenate at the suffix itself:

plan-ning

run-ning

driv-ing

call-ing

8. Never put the first or last letter of a word at the end or beginning of a line, and don't put two-letter suffixes at the beginning of a new line:

lovely (Do not separate in a way which leaves *ly* beginning a new line.)

eval-u-ate (Separate only on either side of the u; do not leave the initial e- at the end of a line.)

Punctuation Practice Test

INSTRUCTIONS: For questions 1-18 below, correct all punctuation errors by writing in the correct marks in their correct places. Some sentences only need basic punctuation, like apostrophes and periods; others require more complex forms, such as dashes, hyphens, colons, and ellipses.

1. The paper was clear pertinent and well written
2. Harry and Donnas honeymoon was just as frantic as their wedding
3. She won the race easily in fact she set a state record
4. I am recalling his story I believe as accurately as I can
5. The last year of the twentieth century is 2000 not 99
6. I expected a package this morning however I waited all day for it to arrive
7. Rainy days arent all that bad they provide the water crucial for all life
8. She witnessed a crime on her street she promptly locked her doors
9. We traveled to Rome Italy Athens Greece and Paris France
10. Shakespeare said it best Alls well that ends well
11. He is not well- liked although he says he is everyones friend
12. Sarah she had always loved animals took in the stray kitten
13. Certainly you may borrow my book Gary
14. The 1950s singer Patty Paige sang the novelty song How Much is That Doggie in the Window
15. Nearly all Americans own a Bible but few including scholars of literature have read it
16. Hmmm its a tough decision but Ill take the red one
17. Tuesday July 25 1967 is my birthday
18. I do the laundry make dinner and pick up the kids I should receive a medal for all of these chores

Punctuation Practice Test #2

INSTRUCTIONS: Add ending punctuation.

1. Alas, poor Bill

2. Do you recall in the last grammar exercise, how he fell from his horse

3. You may remember that he cracked his skull as he landed on the rocky ground

4. Shall we resume the story

5. I seized Bill's lifeless wrist and felt for a pulse

6. Nothing

7. How could he have died so easily, by merely falling from a horse

8. What was I going to do

9. It was such a God-forsaken place

10. Help was at least a day's ride away

11. Suddenly I became aware of the large, icy drops of rain on the wind

12. There was nothing else I could do

13. I would have to make camp for the night

14. And what a very long and very cold night it was going to be

PRONOUN AGREEMENT

Rules for Finding and Fixing Pronoun Agreement Errors

Understand the problem.

Whenever you use a *personal pronoun* like **she**, **it**, or **they**, you first have to have an *antecedent*, the word that the pronoun is replacing.

Read this sentence:

> *Gustavo* slowed to the speed limit when *he* saw the police cruiser in the rearview mirror.

The pronoun **he** replaces **Gustavo**. Pronouns like **he** will keep you from repeating **Gustavo, Gustavo, Gustavo** over and over again.

The pronoun must agree with its antecedent. To navigate this agreement successfully, you will need to know these singular and plural pronoun forms:

Singular	Plural
he, she, it	they
him, her, it	them
his, her, hers, its	their, theirs
himself, herself, itself	themselves

The general rule for pronoun agreement is straightforward: A singular antecedent requires a singular pronoun; a plural antecedent needs a plural pronoun.

Read these examples:

> The **boy** scratched **his** armpit.

> The **boys** scratched **their** armpits.

In most cases, you won't need to debate whether you need the singular or plural form. The spoken English you have heard will help you make the right pronoun choice when you write.

Use the correct pronoun in tricky situations.

English unfortunately includes some *special* agreement situations. These will require your more careful attention.

KNOW HOW EACH AND EVERY CAN COMPLICATE PRONOUN AGREEMENT.

In math, 1 + 1 = 2. This rule applies to pronoun agreement as well. If you have 1 singular noun + 1 singular noun, then together they = 2 things, or a plural antecedent.

Read these examples:

> The woodpecker *and* his mate tried *their* best to oust the squirrel who had stolen *their* nest.

> Ronald wanted the attention of the cheerleader *and* the baton twirler, but he could not make *them* look his way.

The plural pronouns **their** and **them** are logical and ear-pleasing choices for **woodpecker + mate** and **cheerleader + baton twirler**, respectively.

Two words, however, have incredible sentence power. **Each** and **every** are singular and can strong-arm an otherwise plural antecedent to become singular as well.

Watch what happens:

> The cowboy *and* his horse drank *their* fill at the desert oasis.

> *Each* cowboy and horse drank *his* fill at the desert oasis.

> *Every* cowboy, horse, pack mule, trail hand, and cook drank *his* fill at the desert oasis.

Each and **every** will also change the verbs that have to agree:

> Whenever a diner walks in five minutes before closing, the cook *and* waitress *sigh* and *roll* their eyes.

Whenever a diner walks in five minutes before closing, every cook and waitress sighs and rolls *her* eyes.

UNDERSTAND HOW CORRELATIVE CONJUNCTIONS CAN CONFUSE PRONOUN AGREEMENT.

Exercise caution when you use *correlative conjunctions* like **either ... or**, **neither ... nor**, and **not only ... but also**. Because correlative conjunctions have two parts, you'll find two separate antecedents.

Read these examples:

> <u>Not only</u> the *handpicked flowers* <u>but also</u> the *homemade peanut butter pie* will win Briana's heart with *its* thoughtfulness.

> <u>Not only</u> the *homemade peanut butter pie* <u>but also</u> the *handpicked flowers* will win Briana's heart with *their* thoughtfulness.

Notice that you have two antecedents, the **homemade peanut butter pie** and the **handpicked flowers**. Use the *closer* of the two antecedents to determine if you need a singular or plural pronoun.

RECOGNIZE THE PROBLEMS THAT SINGULAR INDEFINITE PRONOUNS CAN CAUSE.

Indefinite pronouns, a special class of words, will often be antecedents. Some indefinite pronouns—despite the illogic—are always singular:

SINGULAR INDEFINITE PRONOUNS
each, either, neither
anybody, anyone, anything
everybody, everyone, everything
nobody, no one, nothing
somebody, someone, something

When people talk, logic wins, so you will hear plural pronouns with these words. But when you write, words like **everyone, somebody,** and **nothing** are singular and require a singular pronoun for agreement.

30

> *Everyone* on the planet deserves clean water to quench ~~their~~ *his* thirst.
>
> Can you believe it? *Somebody* left ~~their~~ *her* dog in a hot car with the windows rolled up!
>
> *Nothing* is in ~~their~~ *its* place after the violent shaking from the earthquake.

Because this group of indefinite pronouns is singular, your choice of singular pronoun might strike some people as sexist. If, for example, you say,

> *Everybody* should take *his* seat.

then the females present might take offense that you have excluded *them*. Or if you say,

> *No one* needs *her* money because the food is free.

then the males might wonder why *they* have to pay.

One solution is to include both genders with constructions like **he or she**, **him or her**, **his or hers**, or **him or herself**.

The problem with using these inclusive constructions is that they are awkward. Although you do maintain pronoun agreement and avoid offending one gender, these constructions wreck the cadence of a good sentence.

Read a piece of professional writing—an essay, a movie or book review, an opinion piece in the newspaper—and you'll notice that real writers, those folks who engage audiences that number in the thousands or millions, will seldom, if ever, use a phrase like **he or she**.

Instead, professional writers might revise the sentence so that a pronoun is unnecessary. Sometimes, they make the antecedent plural so that they can use the natural-sounding **they**, **them**, or **their**. Or they might decide to alternate **he** and **she** in the piece so that both genders get mentioned.

Using **he or she** or **him or her** is *technically* correct. But it's also bad style. Avoid these constructions if you can.

REALIZE THAT NOT ALL INDEFINITE PRONOUNS ARE STRICTLY SINGULAR.

Another group of indefinite pronouns are singular or plural, depending on the information from the *prepositional phrase* that follows.

INDEFINITE PRONOUNS THAT CAN BE SINGULAR OR PLURAL
all, any, none*, more, most, some

Read these examples:

Some of this footwear smells because Tina wears *it* to the barn.

Some of these shoes smell because Tina wears *them* to the barn.

In the first sentence, **footwear** makes **some** singular, so **it** is the pronoun that agrees. In the second sentence, **shoes**, a plural noun, has all the power. **Some** becomes plural too, and **them** is the appropriate pronoun for agreement.

*Some people consider **none** a strictly singular word, a contraction of **no one**. We at *Grammar Bytes!* subscribe to the alternative belief that **none** is the opposite of **all**, and, like **all**, can be either singular or plural. Exercises here will reflect that belief.

KNOW HOW TO HANDLE PRONOUN AGREEMENT WITH COLLECTIVE NOUNS.

Collective nouns name groups [things] composed of members [usually people].

Here are examples:

COLLECTIVE NOUNS
army, audience, board, cabinet, class committee, company, corporation, council department, faculty, family, firm, group

> jury, majority, minority, navy
> public, school, senate, team, troupe

When the members of the group act *in unison*—everyone doing essentially the same thing at the same time—then the collective noun is singular and requires singular pronouns for agreement.

Read these examples:

> The *family* is at the table, ready for *its* dinner, when Grandma prepares her delicious chicken pot pie.
>
> The *committee* decided to spend *its* budget on surplus yo-yos for the officers.
>
> The *team* agreed to host a car wash to finance *its* farthest away game.

When, however, the members of the group act *as individuals*—each person taking on separate responsibilities or actions—then the collective noun is plural and requires plural pronouns for agreement.

Look what happens:

> When Grandpa begins boiling liver, the *family* quickly find other plans for *their* dinner.
>
> At the car wash, the *team* took *their* places so that each vehicle got vacuumed, washed, and dried.
>
> The *committee* disagree if *they* should offer Billie financial assistance after he suffered a concussion during an unfortunate yo-yo accident.

If deciding whether the collective noun is singular or plural makes your head hurt, remember that you have a couple of options.

First, you can substitute a regular plural noun for the collective noun. Then you can use a natural-sounding plural pronoun.

> The ~~team~~ *football players* [or *athletes*, or *teammates*] earned 500 dollars for *their* trip.

Another option is to add the word **members** after a collective noun. **Members** is a plural antecedent and requires an ear-pleasing plural pronoun.

When Grandpa has dinner duty, the family *members* stretch *their* budgets eating dollar items from the value menu at Tito's Taco Palace.

The committee *members* wish that *they* had spent *their* surplus on soft teddy bears, not skull-crushing yo-yos.

UNLIKE COLLECTIVE NOUNS, NAMED BUSINESSES, SCHOOLS, AND ORGANIZATIONS ARE ALWAYS SINGULAR.

Many people comprise a business, school, or organization. For the purposes of pronoun agreement, however, consider these three groups singular and use *it*, *its*, or *itself* to maintain agreement.

Read these examples:

To increase *its* profits, *Tito's Taco Palace* packs *its* burritos with cheap refried beans.

Weaver High School encourages *its* students to make leaner lunch choices, such as hot, steaming bowls of squid eyeball stew.

The Southeastern Association of Salt & Pepper Shaker Enthusiasts will hold *its* annual convention in Atlanta.

Pronoun-Antecedent Agreement Worksheet

Some of the following sentences contain a problem with pronoun-antecedent agreement. Mark the correct sentences "OK" and edit the incorrect ones to eliminate the problem.

1. Each college student brings experience to their classes.

2. Derek and Daniel think that they saw a ghost, but he is not sure.

3. Posted signs around campus are advising people to wash their hands to avoid the spread of flu germs.

4. Everyone who drew a ticket from the pool will receive his or her reward.

5. The ones who texted during the class will be reprimanded for their actions.

6. Carly decided that Carmen would help. She was pleased with the decision.

7. Once a month the group would deliver goods to their community's food bank.

8. Wal-Mart competes with Amazon, but surveys show that it is winning the competition.

9. Jewels covered the criminal's apartment and proved of his guilt.

10. No one could believe their eyes when they saw the pile of money!

Directions: In the space provided, fix the underlined error.

_____1. Nobody knows that eating chocolate-broccoli muffins is a good way to provide their bodies with vitamin C.

_____2. The troupe of knife jugglers shocked their audience when a butcher knife accidentally decapitated the head of an old woman's poodle.

_____3. Either the grill crew or the manager must give their permission for you to return that half-eaten double cheeseburger.

_____4. Both the computer monitor and the refrigerator door have its shiny surface smeared with dog snot from our curious puppy Oreo.

_____5. Which member of your track team makes their opponents resemble turtles trying to compete with a hare?

_____6. The catering committee for the Halloween dance received many compliments for their squid eyeball stew.

_____7. The new and improved laundry detergent restored Hector's mud-stained pants to its original condition.

_____8. After feeding several quarters into the gumball machine, a person learns that they have little chance of receiving the miniature camera in the display.

_____9. Mrs. Carson, like every other American literature teacher, has their own interpretation of the symbols in Moby-Dick.

_____10. Every puppy and kitten will cry at night until their owner comes to carry it to bed.

DANGLING & MISPLACED MODIFIERS

Dangling and Misplaced Modifiers

A modifier is a wonderful tool. Without modifiers, you could never say that a *pretty* girl took home a *happy* dog or that a *nice* boy bought a *yummy* popsicle. In case you didn't get it from the italics, a modifier is a word or phrase that provides more information about something being discussed in the sentence. Modifiers are usually adjectives (words that describe nouns or pronouns) or adverbs (words that describe verbs, adjectives and other adverbs).

Although modifiers can be great, sometimes they can also get lost or put in the wrong place in a sentence. When this happens, things can get very confusing! The following worksheet demonstrates some misplaced and dangling modifiers. Some additional links are also provided to additional worksheets to help make sure you *really* understand the concept!

Examples of Misplaced or Dangling Modifiers

A misplaced modifier is in a modifier that is in the wrong place. For example:

- The pretty girl fast ran. *Fast* is modifying girl, so it is misplaced.

- Hoping it would rain, the umbrella was brought by Ann. *Hoping it would rain* is modifying Ann, since Ann is the person who was hoping it would rain. As written, this sentence makes it sound as though the umbrella was hoping it would rain. While an umbrella might very well hope for such a thing, umbrellas aren't really capable of hoping and so the sentence is illogical.

A dangling modifier modifies something that never actually appears in the sentence. For example:

- Hoping it would rain, the umbrella was brought. In this sentence, there isn't a single person mentioned who has the ability to hope it would rain. The subject being modified is missing entirely and the modifier is left dangling all by itself.

Worksheet for Misplaced or Dangling Modifiers

Now that we have reviewed what a misplaced and dangling modifier is, here is a quick worksheet to help you grasp the concept.

Five sentences are listed below. Label whether the sentence is a misplaced modifier (M), a dangling modifier (D) or correct.

1. Always eager for cake, the birthday party was attended by everyone.

2. Forgetting that the microphone was on, the whole audience heard the singer's fight with his wife.

3. Wagging her tail, the new puppy climbed into my lap.

4. After painting all day, the bright new watercolor was drying in the sunshine.

5. Late as always, Mike made quite an entrance when he came to the party.

Active vs. Passive Voice

Active Voice v. Passive Voice

The term voice, when used in English grammar, refers to the structure of a sentence. There are two "voices" in English grammar, active voice and passive voice.

Active Voice: In an active voice sentence, the agent (the one who does the action in the sentence) is stated explicitly as the grammatical subject. The thing that the agent does something to (the direct object) comes after the verb. Here's an example.

Active Voice Sentence: Julio cooked fried rice.

"Julio" is the agent. He's the one who does the action. In this case, he's the one who cooked the rice.

In this active voice sentence, Julio is the grammatical subject. What did Julio cook? He cooked fried rice. The words fried rice make up the direct object. The fried rice is the thing that the agent (Julio) does something to. In this case he cooked it.

Passive Voice: In a passive voice sentence, the thing that the agent does something to is placed as the grammatical subject of the sentence. The agent (the one who does the action) is placed after the subject, usually in a prepositional phrase. In fact, sometimes the agent is hidden, not even mentioned.

Passive Voice Sentence: The fried rice was cooked by Julio. (The agent is mentioned.)

Passive Voice Sentence: The fried rice was cooked. (The agent is not mentioned.)

In Business Writing, use the Active Voice. Use the active voice in most of the writing you do in school and at work. Studies in readability indicate that active voice sentences, where the agent is stated first, are easier to understand than passive voice sentences.

So When Should You Use the Passive Voice?

1. When the receiver of the action is more important than the agent.

Active Voice: The Nobel Foundation awarded President Obama the Nobel Peace Prize.

Passive Voice: President Obama was awarded the Nobel Peace Prize.

The passive voice construction places the emphasis on the receiver of the Nobel Peace Prize, not on the organization that awarded the prize.

2. When you consciously try to minimize the role of the agent or the agent is not known.

Active Voice: Marie Jenkins could not complete the status report because James McDonald misplaced the manufacturing data.

Passive Voice: The status report was not completed because manufacturing data were misplaced.

3. When you write about scientific, technical, or natural processes.

Active Voice: The conveyor belt delivers the shrink-wrapped product to the packing station.

Passive Voice: The shrink-wrapped product is delivered to the packing station.

Using active voice or passive voice is a stylistic and rhetorical choice about sentence structure. It's important to understand the structure so that you control the structure instead of letting the structure control you. But remember; use the active voice in most of your academic and work-related writing.

Exercises: Convert each sentence from active to passive or from passive to active. Justify your decision.

1. When the Phillies's Shane Victorino overran him, third base was stolen by Johnny Damon.

2. A happy Thanksgiving is wished by me for everyone.

3. The attorney general indicted the notorious gangster, Al Capone, for federal income tax evasion.

4. The student services committee forwarded revised disciplinary procedures to the campus president.

5. Six Thousand shares of Disney stock were bought by Jenny Allen when she was only nineteen.

6. People can view the dazzling meteor shower from the observation tower at the planetarium.

7. The acceptance letter from Harvard was received by Jenny Arteaga last Tuesday.

8. An invitation to Francis Suarez's victory party was received by Mr. Packer, the state party chairman.

PARTS OF SPEECH GUIDELINES

English Grammar 101: The 8 Parts of Speech

Does the thought of learning English grammar cause your eyes to glaze over? If so, it's hard to blame you. Grammar is typically understood to be a set of rules governing a language; its parts of speech, varying voices and tenses, and different articles, among others–not the most exciting topic in the world, is it? For the most part, it's intuitive, especially if English is your first language. However, if you were asked to tell the difference between demonstrative pronouns and interrogative pronouns, could you do it?

English grammar can seem dry and complex, but with a little guidance, it can be easy to digest. Grammar is absolutely essential if you're thinking of breaking into writing, and it's good to know for other reasons, too. Besides making you look positively studious and giving you excellent communication skills, knowing basic grammar rules–Grammar 101, if you will–**can help you learn other languages**, too, since you'll already be familiar with the way that language changes.

The 8 (and sometimes 9) Parts of Speech

For our purposes, grammar 101 will explore the 8 (and sometimes 9–we'll go over that in a while) parts of speech, or lexical categories, if you're feeling especially academic. Now, in English, you can break these categories down even further, but given this is Grammar 101, we're going to stick to the very basics.

1. Nouns

A noun is the largest lexical class, and it's usually the first thing children learn. Why? Nouns are basic: they describe a person, place, or thing. Let's look at a few sentences–note that all of the nouns in the sentences have been bolded:

The **duck** swims on the placid **pond**.

Mandarin Ducks mate for **life**.

My **mother** always told **me**, "a **stitch** in **time** saves **nine**."

Some basic rules of thumb to remember with nouns is that these are the words that can be pluralized (duck, ducks), made possessive (that man's sister), and changed with a prefix or suffix like -age or -hood in order to change it to a new verb (sister/sisterhood, sign/signage). While this doesn't apply to all nouns, it's a great place to start. Also remember that proper nouns, a subclass of nouns, are always capitalized. For instance: New York, Mrs. Smith, University of Texas.

2. Pronoun

Pronouns constitute a rather small lexical class, but they can also be the most confusing. That's because as a pronoun can take so many forms. They exist in the first, second, and third person, and are further classified into nominative, oblique, reflexive, possessive determiners, and possessive pronouns. If you can believe it, they can be broken down even further than that. But for the purposes of keeping grammar 101 simple, let's stick to those essential categories, written in the same order as above.

- **First Person**:
    - I
    - me
    - myself
    - my
    - mine
- **Second Person** (singular and plural):
    - you/y'all/you all
    - you/ya'll/you all
    - yourself/yourselves
    - your
    - yours
- **Third Person**:
    - he/she/they/it
    - him/her/they/it
    - herself/himself/themself/itself
    - her/his/their/it
    - hers/his/theirs
- **First Person Plural**:
    - we
    - us
    - ourselves
    - our
    - ours
- **Third Person Plural**:
    - they
    - them
    - themselves
    - their
    - theirs

3. Determiner

Determiners are another relatively small lexical class, consisting mainly of articles and a few demonstrative and interrogative words. In other languages, articles may be gendered. For instance: in French the article *la* precedes a feminine noun, and *le* precedes a masculine one. In English, because nouns are not gendered, the most common determiner used in English grammar is the word "the". Let's look at a few of the ways determiners are used. In these sentences, the determiner will again be bolded for clarity:

- Basic Determiner: Mike ate **an** apple.
- Quantifying Determiner: Mike ate **many** apples.
- Possessive Determiner: **Mike's** apple was delicious.

You can see that determiners are necessary because it simply does not make sense to say "Mike ate apple", right? There are some other instances where either pronouns or numerals can serve as determiners as well, for instance:

- Pronoun Determiner: **His** apples were not ripe.
- Numeral Determiner: **Four** apples were rotten.

Of course, like most rules in English grammar, the determiner rule can be broken. However, there aren't many situations where this acceptable, and generally only applies if you are referring to a large group or class of things. In that instance, you would say something like, "Unicorns don't exist."

4. Adjective

In Grammar 101, the adjective is the part of speech that gives a sentence the flair it needs, **and they are absolutely essential to great creative writing**. These are descriptive words, and modify a word–usually by being placed in front of it–by describing, identifying, or quantifying it. Here are a few common examples:

The sky turned **dark** and **ominous**.
Gray clouds rolled in, and rain splattered the window.
Sarah put her **polka-dotted** rain boots on.

You can see how adjectives are used in English grammar to add "flavor" to nouns and other words in order to describe them more aptly to the reader or listener.

5. Verb

Next to nouns, verbs comprise the next largest lexical family and are commonly known as "action words" because they help make an assertion regarding what is being done to the subject in a sentence. We'll look at some ways that singular verbs are used below, and then we will take a look at some compound verbs in action.

Lily **ran** to the store to **buy** some apples.
The dog **snarled** at the burglar.

These verbs are singular, in that they require no additional word to describe the action taking place in the sentence. Compound verbs are made up of a singular verb and an auxiliary verb to help determine the tense of an action. Auxiliary verbs are commonly known as "helping verbs" for this very reason. Let's see how compound verbs look in a sentence. The entire compound verb will be bolded, and the auxiliary verb will be underlined.

Lily **<u>will</u> run** to the store to buy some apples.
The dog **<u>was</u> snarling** at the burglar.

You can see that in the above examples, "will" is used to help determine the future tense of the verb "run", and that the auxiliary verb "was" modifies "snarl". It becomes "snarling", which helps determine that the action took place in the past.

6. Adverbs

A regular adverb serves one purpose: they modify verbs, adjectives, clauses and phrases. You can think of it as a kind of hybrid between a verb and an adjective. Unlike an adjective, the adverb can be placed anywhere in a sentence. Adverbs typically (but not always) end with the suffix "-ly" and can answer the questions "where, when, how, and how much?" Let's take a look:

Blake sharpened his pencil as **quietly** as possible.
The child swings her legs **impatiently**.
Fortunately, we will have enough pizza for everyone.

In the above sentences, we see how the adverb works as a modifier. In the first, "quietly" modifies the verb "sharpened." in the second, "impatiently" modifies the verb "swings", and in the last sentence, "Fortunately" modifies the entire phrase. You can also see from these examples how an adverb can be placed anywhere in a sentence, and how it does not change even as the tense changes.

Of course, there are a few "unofficial" grammar rules regarding the use of adverbs. For instance, some consider it bad form to end a sentence with an adverb. There are also multiple instances in which an adverb can also serve as a conjunction, a speech part that we'll explore in a moment. Beyond grammar 101, **a more in-depth look at advanced grammar rules and nuances can help you to understand some of these adverb exceptions**.

7. Prepositions

Prepositions are linking words; they introduce the object of the preposition in a word or phrase. They also address the spatial or temporal location of the words that they introduce, in other words, where an object exists in space or time. Like pronouns, they are a closed class of lexical elements:

Sarah looked **everywhere** for her book and found it **under** the couch.
Marc checked his text messages **during** his lunch break.
Stefan was well known **throughout** the academic community; he was lauded for his grammar prowess.

In these examples, you can see how prepositional phrases and stand-alone prepositions link words together in the sentence, and how they can be used to introduce an object.

8. Conjunctions

Conjunctions are like super-prepositions. Instead of linking just words, they can link entire phrases, clauses, or sentences. They also fall into three main categories; coordinating, subordinating, and correlative conjunctions. Let's take a moment to look at all three categories:

- **Coordinating Conjunctions**: These types of conjunctions are used to link two independent clauses. In other words, if you remove the conjunction, the two clauses that it links can stand on their own as complete sentences.
    - Sheena took the train, **and** Anna bought a plane ticket.
    - Van Gogh was a brilliant artist, **but** he suffered from clinical depression.
- **Subordinating Conjunctions**: Subordinating conjunctions are used to link an independent clause to a clause that cannot stand on its own. These are called dependent clauses because they require an independent clause in order to make sense in the context of the sentence.
    - **If** the plumber comes on Friday, you can finally take a shower.
    - We checked beneath the couch cushions, **where** loose change often falls.
- **Correlative Conjunctions:** You will recognize correlative conjunctions as a set of two words that are rarely used independently of one another. They serve to illustrate cause and effect or to make a general correlation between two clauses:
    - **Either** she will take the trash out, **or** the kitchen will start to stink.
    - **If** her mother gives permission, **then** Jane will stay out late.

Whew! We're *this* close to wrapping up grammar 101, which will hopefully leave you with a better understanding of how the 8 parts of speech are broken down. As promised, we'll touch very briefly on the 9th part of speech. Some argue that because this final category is almost always used independently, it doesn't really count as a proper lexical family. We decided to include it anyway because it's the simplest part of speech to understand. Why not end grammar 101 on an easy-peasy lesson?

9. Interjections

Interjections are the little pieces of language that add emotion to speech or writing. They usually end with an exclamation point, leaving them grammatically unrelated to the rest of the sentence, or they can be incorporated into a larger sentence, usually at the beginning or end of a phrase.

"**Ouch!**" Tamara cried.

Oh no, is that bill due today?

So you're going to go through with it, **eh**?

See? Easy and arguably the most fun lexical categories.

101+ POWER VERBS

1. **Accommodate:** to make fit, suitable, or congruous: to bring into agreement or concord : RECONCILE: to provide with something desired, needed, or suited (as a helpful service, a loan, or lodgings): to make room for: to hold without crowding or inconvenience: to give consideration to : allow for *accommodate the special interests of various groups*ADAPT, CONTAIN
2. **Achieve:** to carry out successfully : ACCOMPLISH *achieve a gradual increase in production*: to get or attain: REACH *achieved a high degree of skill* *achieved greatness*: to attain a desired end or aim : become successful: PERFORM
3. **Acquire:** to get as one's own: to come into possession or control of often by unspecified means: to come to have as a new or added characteristic, trait, or ability (as by sustained effort or natural selection) *acquire fluency in French* *bacteria that acquire tolerance to antibiotics*: to locate and hold (a desired object) in a detector *acquire a target by radar*
4. **Adapt:** to make fit (as for a specific or new use or situation) often by modification: to ADJUST, ACCOMMODATE, CONFORM, RECONCILE. ADAPT implies a modification according to changing circumstances *adapted themselves to the warmer climate
5. **Affect:** to produce an effect upon: to produce a material influence upon or alteration in *paralysis affected his limbs*: to act upon (as a person or a person's mind or feelings) so as to effect a response : INFLUENCE
6. **Affirm:** VALIDATE, CONFIRM: to state positively: to assert (as a judgment or decree) as valid or confirmed: to express dedication to: to testify or declare by affirmation as distinguished from swearing an oath. Conviction based on evidence, experience, or faith.
7. **Alter:** to make different without changing into something else: to become different :CHANGE
8. **Analyze:** to study or determine the nature and relationship of the parts of by analysis *analyze a traffic pattern* DISSECT, BREAK DOWN
9. **Anticipate:** to give advance thought, discussion, or treatment to: to meet (an obligation) before a due date: to foresee and deal with in advance : FORESTALL: to act before (another) often so as to check or counter: to look forward to as certain : EXPECT: FORESEE
10. **Assert:** to state or declare positively and often forcefully or aggressively: to demonstrate the existence of : DECLARE, AFFIRM,
11. **Benefits:** to be useful or profitable to: to receive benefit
12. **Cease:** : to cause to come to an end especially gradually : no longer continue: to come to an end: to bring an activity or action to an end : DISCONTINUE: to become extinct : DIE OUT: STOP
13. **Challenge:** to dare, to protest, to provoke, to stimulate, to question
14. **Characterize:** to describe the character or quality of *characterizes him as ambitious*: to be a characteristic of : DISTINGUISH *an era characterized by greed*
15. **Clarify:** to free of confusion: to make understandable: to become clear

16. **Coincide:** to occupy the same place in space or time: : to correspond in nature, character, or function: to be in accord or agreement : CONCUR: AGREE
17. **Compel:** to drive or urge forcefully or irresistibly: to cause to do or occur by overwhelming pressure: to drive together: FORCE
18. **Compliments:** to pay a compliment to: to present with a token of esteem
19. **Condemn:** to declare to be reprehensible, wrong, or evil usually after weighing evidence and without reservation: to pronounce guilty : CONVICT b : SENTENCE, DOOM: to adjudge unfit for use or consumption: CRITICIZE
20. **Confirm:** to give approval to : RATIFY: to make firm or firmer: STRENGTHEN: to give new assurance of the validity of : remove doubt about by authoritative act or indisputable fact: CORROBORATE, SUBSTANTIATE, VERIFY, AUTHENTICATE, VALIDATE
21. **Conform:** to give the same shape, outline, or contour to : bring into harmony or accord *conform furrows to the slope of the land* : to be similar or identical : to be in agreement or harmony   used with to or with: to be obedient or compliant: to act in accordance with prevailing standards or customs: ADAPT
22. **Confront:** to face especially in challenge : OPPOSE: to cause to meet : bring face-to-face *confront a reader with statistics* b : to meet face-to-face : ENCOUNTER *confronted the possibility of failure*
23. **Console**: to alleviate the grief, sense of loss, or trouble of : COMFORT *console a widow*
24. **Contemplate**: to view or consider with continued attention : meditate on: to view as contingent or probable or as an end or intention: to PONDER, MEDITATE
25. **Contradict**: to assert the contrary of : take issue with: to imply the opposite or a denial of *your actions contradict your words* DENY
26. **Contrast**: to set off in contrast : compare or appraise in respect to differences *contrast European and American manners* to COMPARE
27. **Contribute**: to give or supply in common with others: to play a significant part in bringing about an end or result
28. **Covet**: to wish for enviously: to desire what belongs to another
29. **Criticize**: to consider the merits and demerits of and judge accordingly : EVALUATE: to find fault with : point out the faults of: REPREHEND, CENSURE, REPROBATE, CONDEMN, DENOUNCE
30. **Declare**: to make known formally, officially, or explicitly: to make clear: to make evident : SHOW: to state emphatically : AFFIRM *declares his innocence*: to make a full statement of (one's taxable or dutiable property): to announce (as a trump suit) in a card
31. **Defend**: to maintain or support in the face of argument, to drive danger or attack away from, to prevent, to contest, to take action against or challenge, to PROTECT, SHIELD, GUARD

32. **Demonstrate**: to show clearly: to prove or make clear by reasoning or evidence: to illustrate and explain especially with many examples: to SHOW
33. **Denounce**: to pronounce especially publicly to be blameworthy or evil: PROCLAIM: to announce threateningly: to inform against : ACCUSE: CRITICIZE
34. **Depict**: to represent by or as if by a picture: DESCRIBE
35. **Desire**: to long or hope for : exhibit or feel desire for: to express a wish for : REQUEST: to express a wish to : WISH, WANT, CRAVE, COVET. DESIRE stresses the strength of feeling and often implies strong intention or aim *desires to start a new life*
36. **Disclose**: to open up: to expose to view: to make known or public *demands that politicians disclose the sources of their income*:REVEAL
37. **Displace**: to remove from the usual or proper place: to expel or force to flee from home or homeland: to remove from an office, status, or job: to drive out : BANISH: to move physically out of position *a floating object displaces water* b : to take the place of (as in a chemical reaction) : REPLACE
38. **Display**: to show
39. **Distinguish**: to perceive a difference in : mentally separate *so alike they could not be distinguished*: to mark as separate or different: to separate into kinds, classes, or categories: to give prominence or distinction to *distinguished themselves in music*: CHARACTERIZE: DISCERN *distinguished a light in the distance*: to single out : take special notice of
40. **Dominate**: RULE, CONTROL: to exert the supreme determining or guiding influence on: to overlook from a superior elevation or command because of superior height or position: to have or exert mastery, control, or preeminence
41. **Elate**: to fill with joy or pride
42. **Elevate**: to lift up : RAISE : to raise in rank or status : EXALT: to improve morally, intellectually, or culturally: to raise the spirits of : ELATE
43. **Eliminate**: to cast out or get rid of, to REMOVE, ERADICATE.
44. **Embody**: to give a body to (a spirit) : to make concrete and perceptible: to cause to become a body or part of a body : INCORPORATE: to represent in human or animal form : PERSONIFY *men who greatly embodied the idealism of American life A. M. Schlesinger b1917*
45. **Embrace**: to clasp in the arms : HUG: CHERISH, LOVE: ENCIRCLE, ENCLOSE: to take up especially readily or gladly *embrace a cause*:WELCOME *embraced the opportunity to study further*: to take in or include as a part, item, or element of a more inclusive whole *charity embraces all acts that contribute to human welfare*ADOPT, INCLUDE
46. **Emerge**: to become manifest: to rise from: come out into view: to rise from an obscure or inferior position or condition
47. **Emit**: to throw or give off or out (as light) : to send out : EJECT: to issue with authority: to give utterance or voice to *emitted a groan*

48. **Encounter**: to meet, to engage, to come upon face to face.
49. **Enhance**: RAISE: HEIGHTEN, INCREASE: to increase or improve in value, quality, desirability, or attractiveness
50. **Emphasize**: to place emphasis on : STRESS *emphasized the need for reform*
51. **Enlighten**: : ILLUMINATE: to furnish knowledge to : INSTRUCT: to give spiritual insight to
52. **Enrich**: : to make rich or richer especially by the addition or increase of some desirable quality or attribute *the experience will enrich your life*: to add beauty to : ADORN b : to enhance d : to improve
53. **Evoke**: to call forth or up : CONJURE *evoke evil spirits*: to cite especially with approval or for support : INVOKE: to bring to mind or recollection *this place evokes memories*: to recreate imaginatively
54. **Evolve**: EMIT: DERIVE, EDUCE: to produce by natural evolutionary processes: DEVELOP, WORK OUT
55. **Exceed**: to extend outside of *the river will exceed its banks*: to be greater than or superior to: to go beyond a limit set by *exceeded his authority*: OVERDO, SURPASS, TRANSCEND, EXCEL, OUTDO, OUTSTRIP mean to go or be beyond a stated or implied limit, measure, or degree. EXCEED implies going beyond a limit set by authority or established by custom or by prior achievement *exceed the speed limit*.
56. **Exclude**: to prevent or restrict the entrance of : to bar from participation, consideration, or inclusion: to expel or bar especially from a place or position previously occupied
57. **Exemplify (exemplifies)**: to show or illustrate by example : to make an attested copy or transcript of (a document) under seal: to be an instance of or serve as an example : EMBODY b : to be typical of
58. **Express**: DELINEATE, DEPICT b : to represent in words : STATE c : to give or convey a true impression of : SHOW, REFLECT d : to make known the opinions or feelings of (oneself) e : to give expression to the artistic or creative impulses or abilities of (oneself) f : to represent by a sign or symbol : SYMBOLIZE
59. **Highlight**: to center attention on, to ILLUMINATE, something of major importance.
60. **Identify** : to cause to be or become identical: to conceive as united (as in spirit, outlook, or principle) *groups that are identified with conservation*: to establish the identity of
61. **Illustrate**: a : ENLIGHTEN b : to light up : to make illustrious (1) : to make bright (2) : ADORN 3 a : to make clear : CLARIFY b : to make clear by giving or by serving as an example or instance c : to provide with visual features intended to explain or decorate *illustrate a book*4 : to show clearly : DEMONSTRATE: to give an example
62. **Imitate**: to follow as a pattern, model, or example: to be or appear like : RESEMBLE: to produce a copy of : REPRODUCE: MIMIC, COUNTERFEIT *can imitate his father's booming voice*: COPY

63. **Imply**: to involve or indicate by inference, association, or necessary consequence rather than by direct statement *rights imply obligations*: to contain potentially: to express indirectly *his silence implied consent*: SUGGEST
64. **Impress**: to produce a vivid impression of : to affect especially forcibly or deeply : INFLUENCE
65. **Influence**: the power or capacity of causing an effect in indirect or intangible ways : SWAY: to have an effect on the condition or development of : MODIFY: AFFECT
66. **Indicate**: to point out or point to: to be a sign, symptom, or index of *the high fever indicates a serious condition*: to demonstrate or suggest the necessity or advisability of *indicated the need for a new school*: to state or express briefly *indicated a desire to cooperate*
67. **Interact**: to act upon or among, to socialize.
68. **Interpret**: to explain or tell the meaning of : present in understandable terms: to represent by means of art : bring to realization by performance or direction *interprets a role*
69. **Intervene**: to occur, fall, or come between points of time or events: to come in or between by way of hindrance or modification *intervene to stop a fight*: to interfere usually by force or threat of force in another nation's internal affairs especially to compel or prevent an action: INTERPOSE
70. **Justify**: to prove or show to be just, right, or reasonable b (1) : to show to have had a sufficient legal reason (2) : to qualify (oneself)
71. **Maintain**: to keep in an existing state (as of repair, efficiency, or validity) : preserve from failure or decline *maintain machinery*: to sustain against opposition or danger : uphold and defend *maintain a position*: to continue or persevere in : CARRY ON, KEEP UP *couldn't maintain his composure*: to support or provide for *has a family to maintain* b : SUSTAIN *enough food to maintain life*
72. **Modify**: to make minor changes in: to make basic or fundamental changes in often to give a new orientation to or to serve a new end *the wing of a bird is an arm modified for flying*: to undergo change
73. **Motivate**: to cause to move, to drive someone to action, to spur someone on.
74. **Oblige**: to constrain by physical, moral, or legal force or by the exigencies of circumstance *obliged to find a job* : to put in one's debt by a favor or service *we are much obliged for your help*: to do a favor for *always ready to oblige a friend*
75. **Obtain**: to gain or attain usually by planned action or effort
76. **Oppose**: to place opposite or against something: to place over against something so as to provide resistance, counterbalance, or contrast: to offer resistance to: COMBAT, RESIST, WITHSTAND
77. **Participate**: to possess some of the attributes of a person, thing, or quality: to take part *always tried to participate in class discussions* b : to have a part or share in something: to SHARE

78. **Persecute**: to harass in a manner designed to injure, grieve, or afflict. To cause to suffer because of a belief.
79. **Perceive**: to attain awareness or understanding of: to regard as being such *perceived threats* *was perceived as a loser*: to become aware of through the senses: SEE, OBSERVE
80. **Perseverance/Persevere**: the action or condition or an instance of persevering : STEADFASTNESS. Persevere: to persist in a state, enterprise, or undertaking in spite of counterinfluences, opposition, or discouragement
81. **Ponder**: to weigh in the mind *pondered their chances of success*: to think about : reflect on *pondered the events of the day*: to think or consider especially quietly, soberly, and deeply
82. **Portray**: to make a picture of : DEPICT: to describe in words b : to play the role of : ENACT: to show
83. **Prevent**: to keep from happening or existing *steps to prevent war*: to hold or keep back : HINDER, STOP
84. **Prohibit**: to forbid by authority: to prevent from doing something: PRECLUDE: FORBID
85. **Project**: to devise in the mind : DESIGN: to plan, figure, or estimate for the future *project expenditures for the coming year*: to throw or cast forward : THRUST: to put or set forth : present for consideration: to attribute (one's own ideas, feelings, or characteristics) to other people or to objects *a nation is an entity on which one can project many of the worst of one's instincts
86. **Promote**: to advance in station, rank, or honor : RAISE: to advance (a student) from one grade to the next higher grade: to contribute to the growth or prosperity of : FURTHER *promote international understanding*: to help bring (as an enterprise) into being : LAUNCH:ADVANCE
87. **Rebel**: : opposing or taking arms against a government or ruler: DISOBEDIENT, REBELLIOUS
88. **Reconcile**: to restore to friendship or harmony *reconciled the factions* : SETTLE, RESOLVE *reconcile differences*
89. **Reflect**: to give back or exhibit as an image, likeness, or outline : MIRROR *the clouds were reflected in the water*: to bring or cast as a result *his attitude reflects little credit on his judgment*: to make manifest or apparent : SHOW *the pulse reflects the condition of the heart*: REALIZE, CONSIDER: to think quietly and calmly b : to express a thought or opinion resulting from reflection
90. **Reinforce**: to strengthen or increase by fresh additions *reinforce our troops* *were reinforcing their pitching staff*: to strengthen by additional assistance, material, or support : make stronger or more pronounced *reinforce levees* *reinforce ideas* : to encourage (a response) with a reinforcer: to seek or get reinforcements

91. **Render**: to transmit to another : DELIVER: GIVE UP, YIELD : to furnish for consideration, approval, or information: as (1) : to hand down (a legal judgment) (2) : to agree on and report (a verdict)(1) : GIVE BACK, RESTORE (2) : REFLECT, ECHO c : to give in acknowledgment of dependence or obligation : PAY: to do (a service) for another: MAKE : IMPART: DEPICT (2) : to give a performance of (3) : to produce a copy or version of *the documents are rendered in the original French* (4) : to execute the motions of *render a salute*: to direct the execution of : ADMINISTER

92. **Resolve**: to cause resolution of (a pathological state): to deal with successfully : clear up *resolve doubts* *resolve a dispute*: to find an answer to: to make clear or understandable: to find a mathematical solution of : to reach a firm decision about *resolve to get more sleep* *resolve disputed points in a text*: to work out the resolution of

93. **Restore**: GIVE BACK, RETURN: to put or bring back into existence or use : to bring back to or put back into a former or original state : RENEW

94. **Reveal**: to make known through divine inspiration: to make (something secret or hidden) publicly or generally known *reveal a secret*: to open up to view : DISPLAY *the uncurtained window revealed a cluttered room*DISCLOSE, DIVULGE, TELL

95. **Revolutionize**: to overthrow the established government: to change fundamentally or completely

96. **Significant/Signifies** : the quality of being important : Signify (signifies) - to be a sign of : MEAN: IMPLY: to show

97. **Simulate**: to give or assume the appearance or effect of often with the intent to deceive : IMITATE: to make a simulation of (as a physical system)

98. **Stimulate**: to excite to activity or growth or to greater activity : ANIMATE, AROUSE: PROVOKE

99. **Strengthen**: to make stronger

100. **Surpass**: to become better, greater, or stronger than : EXCEED: to go beyond : OVERSTEP: to transcend the reach, capacity, or powers of EXCEED

101. **Sustain**: to give support or relief to : to supply with sustenance : NOURISH : KEEP UP, PROLONG: to support the weight of : to carry or withstand (a weight or pressure): to buoy up *sustained by hope*: to bear up under: SUFFER, UNDERGO *sustained heavy losses* : to support as true, legal, or just: to allow or admit as valid *the court sustained the motion* : to support by adequate proof : CONFIRM

102. **Symbolize**: to serve as a symbol of: to represent, express, or identify by a symbol

103. **Transcend**: : to rise above or go beyond the limits of: to triumph over the negative or restrictive aspects of : OVERCOME: to be prior to, beyond, and above (the universe or material existence): to outstrip or outdo in some attribute, quality, or power: EXCEED

104. **Transform**: to change in composition or structure: to change the outward form or appearance of : to change in character or condition

TWELVE COMMON WRITING ERRORS

TWELVE COMMON ERRORS: A SELF-EDITING GUIDE

The following list contains only brief examples and explanations intended for you to use as reminders while you are editing your word. To learn more:

1. **Sentence Fragments**. Make sure each word group you have punctuated as a sentence contains a grammatically complete and independent thought that can stand alone as an acceptable sentence.
Incorrect: Tests of the Shroud of Turin have produced some curious findings. For example, the pollen of forty-eight plants native to Europe and the Middle East.
Revised: Tests of the Shroud of Turin have produced some curious findings. For example, the cloth contains the pollen of forty-eight plants native to Europe and the Middle East.
Incorrect: Scientists report no human deaths due to excessive caffeine consumption. Although caffeine does cause convulsions and death in certain animals.
Revised: Scientists report no human deaths due to excessive caffeine consumption, although caffeine does cause convulsions and death in certain animals.

2. **Sentence Sprawl.** Too many equally weighted phrases and clauses produce tiresome sentences.
Incorrect: The hearing was planned for Monday, December 2, but not all of the witnesses could be available, so it was rescheduled for the following Friday. [There are no grammatical errors here, but the sprawling sentence does not communicate clearly and concisely.]
Revised: The hearing, which had been planned for Monday, December 2, was rescheduled for the following Friday so that all witnesses would be able to attend.

3. **Misplaced and Dangling Modifiers.** Place modifiers near the words they describe; be sure the modified words actually appear in the sentence.
Incorrect: When writing a proposal, an original task is set for research [Who is writing a proposal?]
Revised: When writing a proposal, a scholar sets an original task for research.
Incorrect: Many tourists visit Arlington National Cemetery, where veterans and military personnel are buried every day from 9:00 a.m. until 5:00 p.m.
Revised: Every day from 9:00 a.m. until 5:00 p.m., many tourists visit Arlington National Cemetery, where veterans and military personnel are buried.

4. **Faulty Parallelism.** Be sure you use grammatically equal sentence elements to express two or more matching ideas or items in a series.
Incorrect: The candidate's goals include winning the election, a health program, and education.
Revised: The candidate's goals include winning the election, enacting a national health program, and improving the educational system.

Incorrect: Some critics are not so much opposed to capital punishment as postponing it for so long.
Revised: Some critics are not so much opposed to sentencing convicts to capital punishment as they are to postponing executions for so long.

5. **Unclear Pronoun Reference.** Pronouns must clearly refer to definite referents [nouns]. Use it, they, that, these, those, and which carefully to prevent confusion.
Incorrect: Einstein was a brilliant mathematician. This is how he was able to explain the workings of the universe.
Revised: Einstein, who was a brilliant mathematician, used his quantitative ability to explain the workings of universe.
Incorrect: Because Senator Martin is less interested in the environment than in economic development, she sometimes neglects it.
Revised: Because of her interest in economic development, Senator Martin sometimes neglects the environment.

6. **Pronoun Agreement.** Be sure that each pronoun agrees in number (singular or plural) with the noun to which it refers (its antecedent or referent).
Incorrect: When a candidate runs for office, they must expect to have their personal life scrutinized.
Revised: When candidates run for office, they must expect to have their personal lives scrutinized.
Incorrect: According to tenets of the "new urbanism," everyone needs to consider the relationship of their house to the surrounding community.
Revised: According to tenets of the "new urbanism," everyone needs to consider the relationship of his or her house to the surrounding community.

7. **Incorrect Pronoun Case.** Determine whether the pronoun is being used as a subject, object, or possessive in the sentence, and select the pronoun form to match.
Incorrect: Castro's communist principles inevitably led to an ideological conflict between he and President Kennedy.
Revised: Castro's communist principles inevitably led to an ideological conflict between him and President Kennedy.
Incorrect: Because strict constructionists recommend fidelity to the Constitution as written, no one objects more than them to judicial reinterpretation.
Revised: Because strict constructionists recommend fidelity to the Constitution as written, no one objects more than they [object] to judicial reinterpretation.

8. **Omitted Commas.** Use commas to signal nonrestrictive or nonessential material to prevent confusion, and to indicate relationships among ideas and sentence parts.

Incorrect: When it comes to eating people differ in their tastes.
Revised: When it comes to eating, people differ in their tastes.
Incorrect: The Huns who were Mongolian invaded Gaul in 451.
Revised: The Huns, who were Mongolian, invaded Gaul in 451. ["Who were Mongolian" adds information but does not change the core meaning of the sentence because Huns were a Mongolian people; it is therefore nonrestrictive or nonessential and should be set apart with commas.]

9. **Superfluous Commas.** Unnecessary commas make sentences difficult to read.
Incorrect: Field trips are required, in several courses, such as, botany and geology.
Revised: Field trips are required in several courses, such as botany and geology.
Incorrect: The term "scientific illiteracy," has become almost a cliché in educational circles.
Revised: The term "scientific illiteracy" has become almost a cliché in educational circles.

10. **Comma Splice.** Do not link two independent clauses with a comma (unless you also use a coordinating conjunction and, or, but, for, nor, so yet). Instead use a period or semicolon, or rewrite the sentence.
Incorrect: In 1952 Japan's gross national product was one third that of France, by the late 1970s it was larger than the GNPs of France and Britain combined.
Revised: In 1952 Japan's gross national product was one third that of France. By the late 1970s it was larger than the GNPs of France and Britain combined.
Incorrect: Diseased coronary arteries are often surgically bypassed, however half of bypass grafts fail within ten years.
Revised: Diseased coronary arteries are often surgically bypassed; however, half of bypass grafts fail within ten years.

11. **Apostrophe Errors.** Apostrophes indicate possessives and contractions but not plurals. Caution: its, your, their, and whose are possessives (but no apostrophes). It's, you're, they're, and who's are contractions.
Incorrect: In the current conflict its uncertain who's borders their contesting.
Revised: In the current conflict it is [it's] uncertain whose borders they are [they're] contesting.
Incorrect: The Aztecs ritual's of renewal increased in frequency over the course of time.
Revised: The Aztecs' rituals of renewal increased in frequency over the course of time.

12. **Words Easily Confused.** Effect is most often a noun (the effect) and affect is most often a verb. Other pairs commonly confused: lead/led and accept/except. Check a glossary of usage to find the right choice.
Incorrect: The recession had a negative affect on sales.
Revised: The recession had a negative effect on sales. (or) The recession affected sales negatively.
Incorrect: The laboratory instructor choose not to offer detailed advise.
Revised: The laboratory instructor chose not to offer detailed advice.

Essentials of Business Writing Workbook

FUNDAMENTALS OF BUSINESS WRITING

The 10 Fundamentals of Good Business Writing
(excerpt by Tristan Anwyn 08/26/2014)

If you want to communicate more clearly, it's time to master the art of good business writing. To polish your writing and make it a useful tool in any business setting, remember to follow the 10 Cs of good business writing:

Here's what you need to know when putting pen to paper (or fingers to keyboard).

1. **Complete**. It's all too easy to forget that your reader doesn't have the same information as you. A complete message should include all pertinent information – the when, where, why, who and how. You should also include a clear explanation of any action you want your reader to take.

2. **Concise**. Check your writing carefully for redundant words, such as "postpone until later" (you can't postpone until before, so "postpone" is sufficient). Cut out stock phrases such as "I am writing to inform you." A concise message shows the reader that you value their time.

3. **Clear**. Your writing should be clear enough to leave no room for doubt or ambiguity as to what you are trying to say and what action is required. Keep jargon to a minimum and lay out the facts in a logical order.

4. **Conversational**. There's no need to write as if you were writing a legal letter. Write as if you were talking face to face in a friendly but professional tone. Steer clear of slang, but keep your tone warm and remember you are talking to a human being.

5. **Correct**. You only get one chance to make a first impression. That adage is important when it comes to business writing – if your writing is incorrect, your first impression will be sullied. Pay particular attention to: Details such as name and title, correctness in spelling and grammar, correct information and a reader friendly format.

Don't give anyone the written version of the dead fish handshake.

6. **Coherent**. Your reader needs to understand your message immediately. As you set down your thoughts and ideas, do so in a logical manner and help your reader to follow along by linking your ideas together sensibly.

7. **Credible**. Good business writing relies on facts, not opinions. Once lost credibility is hard to repair, so always check your facts and sources. When referencing facts, pay attention to how the data was collected and whether the results were unbiased. Make sure your information is up to date.

8. **Concrete**. Concrete writing means writing that steers clear of vague words and phrases in favor of specifics. For example, "some", "many", "a few", "as soon as possible". These should be replaced with concrete numbers, dates and timescales.

9. **Courteous**. Always put your reader first. Courteous writing includes striving for a positive tone by avoiding commanding phrases such as "you must" and negative phrases such as "you failed". There is no need to strive for false positivity, but taking care over word choice shows consideration for your reader.

10. **Considerate**. Considerate writing means your document is easy to read and scan. You can do this by splitting information into paragraphs with one idea per paragraph, by using bullets and lists for ease of scanning, by using stylistic choices such as bold and italic to emphasize your point, and by using internal headings to guide your reader through the document.

When it comes to business writing, practice really does make perfect. The best business writing process is one that starts with careful planning and ends with careful revision. Whether you are writing a report, a memo, or even a handwritten note, attention to detail and careful choice of words will communicate your point clearly, give a professional impression, and ensure that any requests you make are easily to follow up.

Oral vs. Written Communication

Difference between Oral Communication and Written Communication

Words play a crucial role in communication process, to transmit the message in the way it is intended to be conveyed. When words are used in the process of communication, it is known as verbal communication. Verbal transfer of information can be performed, orally or in written form.

Oral Communication is the oldest means of communication, which is most commonly used as a medium for the exchange of information. It involves gathering or disseminating information through spoken words.

Written Communication, on the other hand, is a formal means of communication, wherein the message is carefully drafted and formulated in written form. It is kept as a source of reference or legal record. In this handout, the important differences between oral and written communication have been noted.

Comparison Chart

BASIS FOR COMMUNICATION	ORAL COMMUNICATION	WRITTEN COMMUNICATION
Meaning	Exchange of ideas, information and message through spoken words is Oral Communication.	Interchange of message, opinions and information in written or printed form is Written Communication.
What is it?	Communication with the help of words of mouth.	Communication with the help of text.
Literacy	Not required at all.	Necessary for communication.
Transmission of message	Speedy	Slow
Proof	No record of communication is there.	Proper records of communication are present.
Feedback	Immediate feedback can be given	Feedback takes time.
Revision before delivering the message?	Not possible	Possible
Receipt of nonverbal cues	Yes	No
Probability of misunderstanding	Very high	Quite less

Definition of Oral Communication

Oral Communication is the process of conveying or receiving messages with the use of spoken words. This mode of communication is highly used across the world because of rapid transmission of information and prompt reply.

Oral communication can either be in the form of direct conversation between two or more persons like face to face communication, lectures, meetings, seminars, group discussion, conferences, etc. or indirect conversation, i.e. the form of communication in which a medium is used for interchange of information like telephonic conversation, video call, voice call, etc.

The best thing about this mode of communication is that the parties to communication, i.e. sender or receiver, can notice nonverbal cues like the body language, facial expression, tone of voice and pitch, etc. This makes the communication between the parties more effective. However, this mode is backed with some limitation like the words once spoken can never be taken back.

Definition of Written Communication

The communication in which the message is transmitted in written or printed form is known as *Written Communication*. It is the most reliable mode of communication, and it is highly preferred in the business world because of its formal and sophisticated nature. The various channels of written communication are letters, e-mails, journals, magazines, newspapers, text messages, reports, etc. There are a number of advantages of written communication which are as under:

- Referring the message in the future will be easy.
- Before transmitting the message, one can revise or rewrite it in an organized way.
- The chances of misinterpretation of message are very less because the words are carefully chosen.
- The communication is planned.
- Legal evidence is available due to the safekeeping of records.

But as we all know that everything has two aspects, same is the case with written communication as the communication is a time consuming one. Moreover, the sender will never know that the receiver has read the message or not. The sender has to wait for the responses of the receiver. A lot of paperwork is there, in this mode of communication.

Wrapping It Up

Oral Communication is an informal one which is normally used in personal conversations, group talks, etc.

Written Communication is formal communication, which is used in schools, colleges, business world, etc.

Choosing between the two communication modes is a tough task because both are good at their places. People normally use the oral mode of communication because it is convenient and less time-consuming. However, people normally believe in the written text more than what they hear that is why written communication is considered as the reliable method of communication.

MISPLACED & DANGLING MODIFIERS

MISPLACED MODIFIERS

A misplaced modifier is a word, phrase or clause that is awkwardly placed in the sentence so that it does not describe what the writer wanted it to describe. In other words, a misplaced modifier is placed so that it does not modify what it is intended to modify.

To avoid this problem, place a modifier as close as possible to the word it modifies.

MISPLACED MODIFIER: Jeff bought an old jeep from a crooked dealer with a faulty transmission.

Did the jeep or the crooked dealer have a faulty transmission? Yes, it was the jeep; therefore, the modifying phrase is awkwardly placed. The phrase with a faulty transmission should be next to the word jeep, the word it modifies.

CORRECTED MODIFIER: Jeff bought an old jeep with a faulty transmission from a crooked dealer.

As you can see, many misplaced modifiers actually cause a sentence to be quite funny; unfortunately, the reader may not have a sense of humor!

MISPLACED MODIFIER: Sam screamed at the barking dog in his underwear.

Now, really, did the dog wear underwear?

CORRECTED EXAMPLE: Sam, in his underwear, screamed at the barking dog.

Modifying words and phrases should be as close as possible to the word they describe, preferably right next to the word they describe. Modifiers may be placed either before or after the word they describe, but the location may change the meaning of the sentence.

MISPLACED MODIFIER: Frances nearly earned fifty dollars.

Frances earned nothing because she just couldn't nearly earn. The modifier must be moved. Frances did not nearly earn; she earned nearly fifty. The modifier nearly is describing how many dollars she earned and thus should be placed next to the word fifty.

CORRECTED EXAMPLE: Frances earned nearly fifty dollars.

Depending on where they are placed in the sentence, the words "nearly" and "only" can change the meaning of a sentence. Consider John and his books:
Only John carried his books to class.
John only carried his books to class.
John carried only his books to class.

DANGLING MODIFIERS

A modifying phrase or clause is said to dangle when it has no stated word to describe. A dangling modifier is sometimes difficult to identify because our brains supply the missing word. To correct a dangling modifier, you must rewrite the sentence and supply the word that is to be modified.

DANGLING MODIFIER: While smoking a pipe, my cat curled up next to me.
Did the cat smoke the pipe? Obviously not, but the sentence does not identify who smoked the pipe. You must supply a subject and, sometimes, supply additional words to create verbs, clauses or phrases. In the following sentences the new subject and additional words are in bold letters.

CORRECTED EXAMPLE: While **I was** smoking a pipe, my cat curled up next to me. OR While smoking a pipe, **I allowed** my cat **to curl** up next to me.

DANGLING MODIFIER: Climbing the mountain, a rock hit John's head.
Who was climbing the mountain? The rock? Jim? We must rewrite the sentence for clarity.

CORRECTED EXAMPLE: When John was climbing the mountain, a rock hit his head. OR Climbing the mountain, John was hit on the head by a rock.

DANGLING MODIFIER: Being out of order, the president asked me to sit down.
Who was being out of order? The president? Me? Rewrite the sentence.

CORRECTED EXAMPLE: Being out of order, I was asked by the president to sit down. OR Because I was out of order, the president asked me to sit down.

EXERCISE 1: First, underline the modifying phrase and circle the word it modifies. Then, rewrite the sentence so that the modifying phrase is as close as possible to the word it describes.

Note: Some sentences contain two modifying phrases.

1. Jack walked into only the house of horrors.
2. She almost needed one day to complete the assignment.
3. Her boyfriend opened the door with a wicked smile.
4. We nearly waited one month for the answer to our questions.
5. My friend took me for a ride after showering and shaving on the skyway.
6. On the way to the movie, a bee stung Dean.
7. The cat should be treated by a veterinarian that has worms.
8. The house in the Arlington area faces the river which Mr. Smith bought.
9. After reaching a weight of 275 pounds, the doctor insisted that Mr. Wright go on a strict diet.
10. Shane washed her hair when she finished eating with a new shampoo.

EXERCISE 2: The following sentences contain dangling modifiers. You will have to supply a subject and rewrite the sentence so that the modifying phrase is in the correct location to describe its subject. Check your answers in the back of this handout.

1. While sweeping the floor, the stew boiled over on the stove.
2. To write correctly, proper English should be used.
3. After putting a new ribbon in the printer, my papers looked better.
4. While washing his brother's car, a scratch was discovered on the bumper.
5. Thinking of something else, the instructor's voice surprised me.
6. While writing my paper, the telephone rang.
7. To understand our new policy, the LAC's brochures were read.
8. Being short of money, an inexpensive restaurant had to be found.
9. On coming back to school after vacation, a new work schedule was developed.
10. By jogging five miles a day a toned body was insured.

COMPOSING THE BASIC BUSINESS LETTER

Writing the Basic Business Letter

Parts of a Business Letter

This resource is organized in the order in which you should write a business letter, starting with the sender's address if the letter is not written on letterhead.

Sender's Address

The sender's address usually is included in letterhead. If you are not using letterhead, include the sender's address at the top of the letter one line below the date. Do not write the sender's name or title, as it is included in the letter's closing. Include only the street address, city, and zip code.

Date

The date line is used to indicate the date the letter was written. However, if your letter is completed over a number of days, use the date it was finished in the date line. When writing to companies within the United States, use the American date format. (The United States-based convention for formatting a date places the month before the day. For example: June 11, 2001.) Write out the month, day and year two inches from the top of the page. Depending which format you are using for your letter, either left justify the date or tab to the center point and type the date.

Inside Address

The inside address is the recipient's address. It is always best to write to a specific individual at the firm to which you are writing. If you do not have the person's name, do some research by calling the company or speaking with employees from the company. Include a personal title such as Ms., Mrs., Mr., or Dr. Follow a woman's preference in being addressed as Miss, Mrs., or Ms. If you are unsure of a woman's preference in being addressed, use Ms. If there is a possibility that the person to whom you are writing is a Dr. or has some other title, use that title. Usually, people will not mind being addressed by a higher title than they actually possess. To write the address, use the U.S. Post Office Format. For international addresses, type the name of the country in all-capital letters on the last line. The inside address begins one line below the sender's address or one line below the date. It should be left justified, no matter which format you are using.

Salutation

Use the same name as the inside address, including the personal title. If you know the person and typically address them by their first name, it is acceptable to use only the first name in the salutation (for example: Dear Lucy:). In all other cases, however, use the personal title and last/family name followed by a colon. Leave one line blank after the salutation.

If you don't know a reader's gender, use a nonsexist salutation, such as their job title followed by the receiver's name. It is also acceptable to use the full name in a salutation if you cannot determine gender. For example, you might write Dear Chris Harmon: if you were unsure of Chris's gender.

Body

For block and modified block formats, single space and left justify each paragraph within the body of the letter. Leave a blank line between each paragraph. When writing a business letter, be careful to remember that conciseness is very important. In the first paragraph, consider a friendly opening and then a statement of the main point. The next paragraph should begin justifying the importance of the main point. In the next few paragraphs, continue justification with background information and supporting details. The closing paragraph should restate the purpose of the letter and, in some cases, request some type of action.

Closing

The closing begins at the same vertical point as your date and one line after the last body paragraph. Capitalize the first word only (for example: Thank you) and leave four lines between the closing and the sender's name for a signature. If a colon follows the salutation, a comma should follow the closing; otherwise, there is no punctuation after the closing.

Enclosures

If you have enclosed any documents along with the letter, such as a resume, you indicate this simply by typing Enclosures one line below the closing. As an option, you may list the name of each document you are including in the envelope. For instance, if you have included many documents and need to ensure that the recipient is aware of each document, it may be a good idea to list the names.

Typist initials

Typist initials are used to indicate the person who typed the letter. If you typed the letter yourself, omit the typist initials.

A Note about Format and Font

Block Format

When writing business letters, you must pay special attention to the format and font used. The most common layout of a business letter is known as block format. Using this format, the entire letter is left justified and single spaced except for a double space between paragraphs.

Modified Block

Another widely utilized format is known as modified block format. In this type, the body of the letter and the sender's and recipient's addresses are left justified and single-spaced. However, for the date and closing, tab to the center point and begin to type.

Semi-Block

The final, and least used, style is semi-block. It is much like the modified block style except that each paragraph is indented instead of left justified.

Keep in mind that different organizations have different format requirements for their professional communication. While the examples provided by the OWL contain common elements for the basic business letter (genre expectations), the format of your business letter may need to be flexible to reflect variables like letterheads and templates. Our examples are merely guides.

If your computer is equipped with Microsoft Office 2000, the Letter Wizard can be used to take much of the guesswork out of formatting business letters. To access the Letter Wizard, click on the Tools menu and then choose Letter Wizard. The Wizard will present the three styles mentioned here and input the date, sender address and recipient address into the selected format. Letter Wizard should only be used if you have a basic understand of how to write a business letter. Its templates are not applicable in every setting. Therefore, you should consult a business writing handbook if you have any questions or doubt the accuracy of the Letter Wizard.

Font

Another important factor in the readability of a letter is the font. The generally accepted font is Times New Roman, size 12, although other fonts such as Arial may be used. When choosing a font, always consider your audience. If you are writing to a conservative company, you may want to use Times New Roman. However, if you are writing to a more liberal company, you have a little more freedom when choosing fonts.

Punctuation

Punctuation after the salutation and closing - use a colon (:) after the salutation (never a comma) and a comma (,) after the closing. In some circumstances, you may also use a less common format, known as open punctuation. For this style, punctuation is excluded after the salutation and the closing.

COMPOSING BUSINESS MEMOS

Crafston Solutions, Inc.
100 N Central, Rowlett, TX 75083
(972) 463 1549

Memo

To: Department Heads
From: Debora Lynn
Date: December 10, 2006
Subject: Annual Bonus Leave for Employees with Outstanding Performane

---

Starting January 1, we will introduce the following modification in our company policy with regard to annual leave: every year one employee from each department will be awarded special annual bonus leave for outstanding performance.

The eligible employees will have additional five (5) days of annual leave credited on January 15. The bonus leave will be accounted for separately and will remain available until used, notwithstanding any other limitation of the total number of days of annual leave that may be carried forward.

We will have a meeting on December 15 at 10:00 a.m. to discuss the results of the 2006 performance evaluation and approve the final list of employees eligible for the bonus. The announcement to the employees will follow the meeting. If you have any questions or comments, please let me know before the meeting.

Audience and Purpose

Memos have a twofold purpose: they bring attention to problems and they solve problems. They accomplish their goals by informing the reader about new information like policy changes, price increases, or by persuading the reader to take an action, such as attend a meeting, or change a current production procedure. Regardless of the specific goal, memos are most effective when they connect the purpose of the writer with the interests and needs of the reader.

Choose the audience of the memo wisely. Ensure that all of the people that the memo is addressed to need to read the memo. If it is an issue involving only one person, do not send the memo to the entire office. Also, be certain that material is not too sensitive to put in a memo; sometimes the best forms of communication are face-to-face interaction or a phone call. Memos are most effectively used when sent to a small to moderate number of people to communicate company or job objectives.

Standard memos are divided into segments to organize the information and to help achieve the writer's purpose.

Heading Segment

The heading segment follows this general format:

TO: (readers' names and job titles)

FROM: (your name and job title)

DATE: (complete and current date)

SUBJECT: (what the memo is about, highlighted in some way)

Make sure you address the reader by his or her correct name and job title. You might call the company president "Maxi" on the golf course or in an informal note, but "Rita Maxwell, President" would be more appropriate for a formal memo. Be specific and concise in your subject line. For example, "Clothes" as a subject line could mean anything from a dress code update to a production issue. Instead use something like, "Fall Clothes Line Promotion."

Opening Segment

The purpose of a memo is usually found in the opening paragraph and includes: the purpose of the memo, the context and problem, and the specific assignment or task. Before indulging the reader with details and the context, give the reader a brief overview of what the memo will be about. Choosing how specific your introduction will be depends on your memo plan style. The more direct the memo plan, the more explicit the introduction should be. Including the purpose of the memo will help clarify the reason the audience should read this document. The introduction should be brief, and should be approximately the length of a short paragraph.

Context

The context is the event, circumstance, or background of the problem you are solving. You may use a paragraph or a few sentences to establish the background and state the problem. Oftentimes it is sufficient to use the opening of a sentence to completely explain the context, such as,

"Through market research and analysis..."

Include only what your reader needs, but be sure it is clear.

Task Segment

One essential portion of a memo is the task statement where you should describe what you are doing to help solve the problem. If the action was requested, your task may be indicated by a sentence opening like,

"You asked that I look at...."

If you want to explain your intentions, you might say,

"To determine the best method of promoting the new fall line, I will...."

Include only as much information as is needed by the decision-makers in the context, but be convincing that a real problem exists. Do not ramble on with insignificant details. If you are having trouble putting the task into words, consider whether you have clarified the situation. You may need to do more planning before you're ready to write your memo. Make sure your purpose-statement forecast divides your subject into the most important topics that the decision-maker needs.

Summary Segment

If your memo is longer than a page, you may want to include a separate summary segment. However, this section not necessary for short memos and should not take up a significant amount of space. This segment provides a brief statement of the key recommendations you have reached. These will help your reader understand the key points of the memo immediately. This segment may also include references to methods and sources you have used in your research.

Discussion Segments

The discussion segments are the longest portions of the memo, and are the parts in which you include all the details that support your ideas. Begin with the information that is most important. This may mean that you will start with key findings or recommendations. Start with your most general information and move to your specific or supporting facts. (Be sure to use the same format when including details: strongest to weakest.) The discussion segments include the supporting ideas, facts, and research that back up your argument in the memo. Include strong points and evidence to persuade the reader to follow your recommended actions. If this section is inadequate, the memo will not be as effective as it could be.

Closing Segment

After the reader has absorbed all of your information, you want to close with a courteous ending that states what action you want your reader to take. Make sure you consider how the reader will benefit from the desired actions and how you can make those actions easier. For example, you might say,

"I will be glad to discuss this recommendation with you during our Tuesday trip to the spa and follow through on any decisions you make."

The format of a memo follows the general guidelines of business writing. A memo is usually a page or two long, should be single spaced and left justified. Instead of using indentations to show new paragraphs, skip a line between sentences. Business materials should be concise and easy to read. Therefore, it is beneficial to use headings and lists to help the reader pinpoint certain information.

You can help your reader understand your memo better by using headings for the summary and the discussion segments that follow it. Write headings that are short but that clarify the content of the segment. For example, instead of using "Summary" for your heading, try "New Advertising Recommendations," which is much more specific. The major headings you choose are the ones that should be incorporated in your purpose-statement in the opening paragraph.

For easy reading, put important points or details into lists rather than paragraphs when possible. This will draw the readers' attention to the section and help the audience remember the information better. Using lists will help you be concise when writing a memo.

The segments of the memo should be allocated in the following manner:

- Header: 1/8 of the memo

- Opening, Context and Task: 1/4 of the memo

- Summary, Discussion Segment: 1/2 of the memo

- Closing Segment, Necessary Attachments: 1/8 of the memo

This is a suggested distribution of the material to make writing memos easier. Not all memos will be the same and the structure can change as you see necessary. Different organizations may have different formatting procedures, so be flexible in adapting your writing skills.

COMPOSING PROFESSIONAL EMAILS

Writing Clear Professional Emails

(Excerpt from David Masters 19 May 2014)

Email is the communication tool of choice for most of us. Email's great because you don't have to be available at the same time as your conversation partner to communicate. It allows us to keep projects moving when our co-workers are unavailable or on the other side of the world.

There's one problem: most of us are drowning in emails. The average person using email for business receives and sends over 100 emails a day, according to a report published by the Radicati Group.

On top of that, emails are all too easily misunderstood. A recent study by Sendmail found that 64% of people have sent or received an email that caused unintended anger or confusion.

Because of the volume of emails we send and receive, and because emails are often misinterpreted, it's important to write emails clearly and concisely.

How to Properly Write a Professional Email (With Clear Points)

Writing emails that are short and to-the-point will reduce the time you spend on email and make you more productive. By keeping your emails short, you'll likely spend less time on email and more time on other work. That said, writing clearly is a skill. Like all skills, you'll have to work at it.

To begin with, it may take you just as long to write short emails as it took you to write long emails. However, even if this is the case, you'll help your co-workers, clients, or employees be more productive because you'll be adding less clutter to their inboxes, making it easier for them to respond to you.

By writing clearly, you'll become known as someone who knows what he or she wants and who gets things done. Both of these are good for your career prospects.

So what does it take to write clear, concise, and professional emails?

Now, let's get into the details of how to write a professional email that will have you writing proper business emails with purpose, clarity, and impact.

1. Know Your Purpose

Clear emails always have a clear purpose.

Whenever you sit down to write an email, take a few seconds to ask yourself: "Why am I sending this? What do I need from the recipient?"

If you can't answer these questions, then you shouldn't be sending an email. Writing emails without knowing what you need wastes your time and the recipient's time and means you'll struggle to express yourself clearly and concisely.

This is also a good time to ask yourself: "Is this email really necessary?" Again, only sending emails that are absolutely necessary shows respect for the person you're emailing.

2. Use the "One Thing" Rule

Emails are not the same as business meetings. With business meetings, the more agenda items you work through, the more productive the meeting.

With emails, the opposite is true. The *less* you include in your emails, the better.

That's why it's a good idea to practice the "one thing" rule. Make each email you send about one thing only. If you need to communicate about another project, write another email.

3. Practice Empathy

Empathy is the ability to see the world through the eyes of other people. When you do this, you understand their thoughts and feelings.

When you write emails, think about your words from the reader's point of view. With everything you write, ask yourself:

- How would I interpret this sentence, as someone reading it?
- How would this make me feel if I received it?

This is a simple tweak to the way you write. Yet thinking of other people will transform the way they respond to you.

Here's an empathetic way of looking at the world to help you get started. Most people:

- Are busy. They don't have time to guess what you want, and they'd like to be able to read and respond to your email quickly.
- Appreciate a compliment. If you can say something positive about them or their work, do so. Your words won't be wasted.
- Like to be thanked. If the recipient has helped you in any way, remember to say thank you. You should do this even when it's their job to help you.

In a moment, we'll look at how you can embed compliments and a thanks into the structure of every email you send.

4. Keep Introductions Brief

When you're emailing someone for the first time, you need to let the recipient know who you are. You can usually do this in one sentence. For example: "It was great to meet you at [X event]." One way of keeping introductions brief is to write them like you're meeting face-to-face. You wouldn't go off into a five-minute monologue when meeting someone in person. So don't do it in email.

Not sure whether an introduction is needed? Maybe you've contacted the recipient before, but you're not sure if she'll remember you. You can leave your credentials in your email signature. This is ideal because:

- It keeps the main email body as short as possible.
- It avoids misunderstandings. Re-introducing yourself to someone who already knows you comes across as rude. If she's not sure whether she knows you, then you can just let her check out your signature.

Talking of signatures, make sure you've set one up. It's a shorthand way of sharing information that you should include in every email. But putting this information in your signature, you keep the body of your emails short.

Your signature should include:

- Your name.
- Your job title.
- A link to your website.

Optionally, you can include links to your social media accounts, and a one-sentence elevator pitch on how you help people.

5. Limit Yourself to Five Sentences

In every email you write, you should use enough sentences to say what you need and no more. A helpful practice here is limiting yourself to five sentences.

Entrepreneur Guy Kawasaki explains:

Less than five sentences is often abrupt and rude, more than five sentences wastes time.

There will be times when it's impossible to keep an email to five sentences. But in most cases, five sentences are sufficient.

Embrace the five sentences discipline, and you'll find yourself writing emails more quickly. You'll also get more replies.

Not sure writing an email in five sentences is possible? Then read on...

6. Stick to a Standard Structure

What's the key to keeping your emails short? Using a standard structure. This is a template that you follow for every email you write.

As well as keeping your emails short, following a standard structure also helps you to write fast. Over time, you'll develop a structure that works for you. Here's a simple structure to get you started:

- greeting
- a compliment or pleasantry
- the reason for your email
- a call to action
- a closing message
- signature

Let's look at each of these in depth.

Greeting. This is the first line of the email. "Hi, [First Name]" is a typical greeting.

Compliment or Pleasantry. When you're emailing someone for the first time, then a compliment makes an excellent opener. A well-written compliment can also serve as an introduction. For example:

- "I enjoyed your presentation about [topic] on [date]."
- "I found your blog post on [topic] really helpful."
- "It was good to meet you at [event]."

If you're writing to someone you know, then use a pleasantry instead. A pleasantry is typically a variation on "I hope you're well." Alternatively, you can say thank you for something they've helped you with or for information they sent in a previous email.

As Vinay Patankar of the *Abstract Living* blog explains:

You should ALWAYS follow with a pleasantry after your greeting. EVERYTIME without fail. Ingrain this into your fingers so that you naturally spit it out with each email you write. There is no reason ever why your email shouldn't have a pleasantry... You will never have anything to lose by adding in a pleasantry, you will make people more inclined to read the rest of your email, you will soften criticism, and will hit the positive emotions of a few. Most will simply ignore it, but for two seconds of your time, it's definitely worth it.

The reason for your email. In this section you say, "I'm emailing to ask about..." or "I wondered if you could help with..." You'll sometimes need two sentences to explain your reasons for writing.

A call to action. After you've explained your reason for emailing, don't assume the recipient will know what to do. Provide specific instructions. For example:

- "Could you send me those files by Thursday?"
- "Could you write that up in the next two weeks?"
- "Please write to James about this, and let me know when you've done so."

Structuring your request as a question encourages the recipient to reply. Alternatively, you can use the line "let me know when you've done that" or "let me know if that's okay with you."

Closing. Before you sign off your email, be sure to include a closing line. This has the dual purpose of re-iterating your call to action, and of making the recipient feel good.

Examples of good closing lines include:

- "Thank you for all your help with this."
- "Does that sound good?"
- "I'm looking forward to hearing what you think."
- "Let me know if you have any questions."

Sign-off. This could be "Best Wishes," "Kind Regards," "All the Best," or "Thanks." You should always follow your sign-off with your name.

7. Use Short Words, Sentences, and Paragraphs

Back in 1946, George Orwell advised writers to:

Never use a long word where a short one will do.

This advice is even more relevant today, especially when writing emails.

Short words show respect for your reader. By using short words, you've done the hard work of making your message easy to understand.

The same is true of short sentences and paragraphs. Avoid writing big blocks of text if you want your email to be clear and easily understood. This leads to another of George Orwell's rules for writing, which can help you keep your sentences as short as possible:

If it is possible to cut a word out, always cut it out.

Once you've followed your standard email structure, trim every sentence down to be as short as it can be.

8. Use the Active Voice

George Orwell again:

Never use the passive where you can use the active.

In writing, there are two kinds of voices, active and passive.

Here's a sentence in the active voice:

I throw the ball.

And here's the same sentence in the passive voice:

The ball is thrown [by me].

The active voice is easier to read. It also encourages *action* and *responsibility*. That's because in the active voice, sentences focus on the person taking action. In the passive voice, sentences focus on the object that's being acted upon. In the passive voice, it can appear that things happen by themselves. In the active voice, things only happen when people take action.

9. Proofread Your Email

The French philosopher Blaise Pascal once said:

If I had more time, I would have written you a shorter letter.

In other words, writing short emails can be harder work than writing long emails.

Part of the hard work of writing short emails is careful proofreading. Read your email aloud to yourself, checking for spelling and grammar mistakes. Ask yourself:
- Is my request clear?
- Could there be any misunderstandings?
- How would this sound if I were the recipient?

Delete any unnecessary words, sentences, and paragraphs as you proofread.

10. Remember, You're Not Fifteen Anymore

If you want to show your personality in your email, let this shine subtly through your writing style. Don't use emoticons, chat abbreviations (such as LOL), or colorful fonts and backgrounds. While these might have been integral to your emails during your teenage years, they are rarely appropriate in a professional context.

The only time it is appropriate to use emoticons or chat abbreviations is when you're mirroring the email language of the person you're writing to. And even then, you should attempt to refrain from such usage.

11. Write Like You Speak

Email is a less formal way of communicating than writing a letter or even making a phone call. Writing as you speak makes you come across as personable and friendly. It also helps you to keep your emails short. After all, few of us speak in extended paragraphs.

Additionally, make sure your emails reflect who you are in the real world. If you wouldn't say something to a person's face, don't say it in an email. And remember to mind your manners. "Please" and "Thank you" go a long way.

PROOFREADING

Review Exercise for Section 33 Use correct spelling and hyphenation.

Correct any misspellings and hyphenation errors.

Recently, researchers who study chimpanzees have come to the suprising conclusion that groups of chimpanzees have their own traditions that can be past on to new generations of chimps. The chimps do not aquire these traditions by instinct; instead, they learn them from other chimps. When a scientific journal published analysises of chimpanzee behavior, the author revealed that the every day actions of chimpanzees in seperate areas differ in significant ways, even when the groups belong to the same subspecies. For instance, in one West African group, the chimps are often seen puting a nut on a stone and using another peice of stone to crack the nut open, a kind of behavior never observed in other groups of chimpanzees. Sceintists have also observed the chimps teaching there young the nut opening method, and chimps in other places that crack nuts differentlly teach their young they're own way. Researchers have therefor concluded that chimpanzees have local traditions.

Frans de Waal, who has been studing primates, wrote a book makeing the arguement that these learned behaviors should be considered kinds of culture. The word culture has traditionly been used to describe human behavier, but may be, he says, a new definition is needed. Considering this startlingly-new theory of chimpanzee "culture," some researchers think that humans now have an un-deniable obligation to protect the lives of all remaining wild chimpanzees rather than zeroeing in on just a few of the threatenned animals. The lost of a single group of wild chimpanzees would, they say, destroy something irreplacable, a unique culture with its own traditions and way of life.

Review Exercise Section 26 Use commas correctly.

Add any necessary commas, delete any that are unnecessary, and replace commas with periods or semicolons as needed.

"All men are created equal" wrote Thomas Jefferson but his deeds did not always match his eloquent words. Like most of the other aristocratic landowners in Virginia, Jefferson the author of the Declaration of Independence founder of the University of Virginia and third president of the United States, owned slaves. One of them was a woman named, Sally Hemings who was one-quarter African, and was probably the daughter of Jefferson's father-in-law and a half-African slave, if this genealogy is correct Hemings was the half-sister of Jefferson's late wife, Martha. Indeed observers at the time noted that, Hemings looked remarkably like Martha Jefferson, who had died on September 6 1782, when Jefferson was thirty-nine.

In 1802 a disgruntled former employee reported that President Jefferson, was the father of Hemings's three children. Jefferson never responded publicly to the charge but, many people noticed the resemblance between him and the Hemings children. The believable scandalous rumors continued to circulate for years after Jefferson's death in 1826. A few historians speculated, that Jefferson's nephews might have fathered the Hemings children but, most ignored the story altogether. Yes it was true that slaveholders had often been known to impregnate slave women, yet such an act was difficult for many white Americans to reconcile with their views of one of the country's founders.

In the 1990s DNA tests were used to determine whether Jefferson could have been the father of Sally Hemings's children. The tests showed a match between the DNA of Jefferson's closest male relative's descendants, and the descendants of Hemings's youngest son, Eston. Clearly either Jefferson or a close relative was Eston's father. Most historians are now convinced that, Jefferson did father at least one of the Hemings children. A recent biography of Jefferson was called American Sphinx and the third president does, indeed seem to have hidden many secrets. Whether the revelations about his relationship with Hemings will change the way Americans feel about this Founding Father, remains to be seen.

Review Exercise for Section 21 Use correct subject-verb agreement.

In the following passage, correct any errors in subject-verb agreement.

There is more people of African descent living in Brazil than in any other country outside of Africa. Although only about ten million of Brazil's 170 million people identifies themselves as black, according to a recent survey, an additional 40 percent of the population call themselves pardo, meaning "dark," or mulato or mestiço, indicating mixed European and African ancestry. There are more than three hundred Brazilian words for skin color, so racial categories in the country is difficult to define. Brazil is a multiracial society that prides itself on avoiding racial divisions like that found in the United States. However, what is clear are that economic and social problems trouble many black Brazilians. Some argue that poor self-image and discrimination based on skin color has contributed to keeping Brazilians from claiming their African ancestry.

The problems of black Brazilians are hard to ignore. Brazil was the last country in the western hemisphere to outlaw slavery. The average income of white-skinned Brazilians are twice the average earnings of blacks. Only 2% of Brazilian college students are black. Brazilian newspaper advertisements for jobs in the private sector often requires applicants to have a "good appearance," a phrase most Brazilians agree is a code for "whites only." Even on television, soap operas and commercials rarely offers roles for black actors. As a solution, the Brazilian Congress have suggested a system of quotas that would require 30% of political candidates, 25% of actors on every television show, 20% of civil service employees, and 20% of college students to be black or of mixed race. Some Brazilians insist that quotas will fail in Brazil, but many hopes that such a quota system will increase opportunity for blacks in the country. Politics do not always provide good solutions for difficult social problems. However, the future of a great number of Brazilians looks bleak unless the country find a way to reduce the problem of racial discrimination.

www.ingramcontent.com/pod-product-compliance
Lightning Source LLC
Chambersburg PA
CBHW081827230426
43668CB00017B/2407